10/10

Fraud in the Markets

Fraud in the Markets

Why It Happens and How to Fight It

PETER GOLDMANN

John Wiley & Sons, Inc.

Published by John Wiley & Sons, Inc., Hoboken, New Jersey.
Published simultaneously in Canada.

For general information on our other products and services or for technical support, please contact our Customer Care Department within the United States at (800) 762-2974, outside the United States at (317) 572-3993 or fax (317) 572-4002.

Wiley also publishes its books in a variety of electronic formats. Some content that appears in print may not be available in electronic books. For more information about Wiley products, visit our web site at www.wiley.com.

Library of Congress Cataloging-in-Publication Data:

Goldmann, Peter, 1953–
    Fraud in the markets: why it happens and how to fight it/Peter Goldmann.
        p. cm.
    Includes index.
    ISBN 978-0-470-50789-6 (cloth)
    1. Capital market.   2. Corporations—Corrupt practices.   I. Title.
    HG4523.G65 2010
    364.16′3—dc22   2009046298

Printed in the United States of America

10 9 8 7 6 5 4 3 2 1

To Barbara and Leah

Contents

Preface

All men are frauds. The only difference between them is that some admit it. I myself deny it.

—H. L. Mencken

This book will examine a wide range of often complex factors that played key roles in bringing the U.S. financial system to the brink of collapse in 2007 and 2008.

Inevitably, the discussion will often have at its core or within its subtext issues related to the subprime mortgage issue.

The reason for this is paradoxically simple: Had there been no subprime mortgage industry—which didn't even get its start until the mid-1980s—there is a good chance that there would have been no financial and economic meltdown.

Some would argue that this is an oversimplified view of the meltdown. They would suggest that because of the culture of greed, hubris, and invincibility on Wall Street, together with a conspicuous absence of government and industry oversight, the rise of the subprime "industry" was inevitable. They would further point out that the subprime problem proved to be only one of *many* financial factors that collectively brought about the worst crisis since the 1930s.

All true. Unfortunately, it is impossible to quantify the exact degree to which each contributing factor catalyzed the financial markets' precipitous demise.

In the end, what really matters is the subprime crisis's related financial failures and how the perfect storm that brought the entire U.S. financial system to its knees came together. Thus, this book will address such issues as:

- The history of the financial markets and the origins of the cultures of greed, financial omnipotence, and hubris that gave rise to a fatal redefinition of risk in the late 1990s and early 2000s.
- The related culture of "anything goes" on Wall Street which fueled the innovation of super-high-risk asset-backed securities whose excessive use went either unaddressed or underestimated to the devastating disadvantage of institutions that invested in them.
- The egregiously fraudulent lending practices that engulfed virtually the entire U.S. mortgage industry, leading to the fatal deterioration of balance sheets and ultimate collapse of major players such as Washington Mutual, Wachovia, Countrywide, as well as untold thousands of unscrupulous mortgage brokers, appraisers, and independent lenders.
- The wildly irresponsible decisions on the part of Wall Street's top honchos that cost them their firms, their jobs and the livelihoods of tens of thousands of their employees and clients.
- The widespread fraudulent marketing of asset-backed securities, based on exaggerated or completely fictitious representations of risk levels, including the stunning indictments of two highly regarded Bear Stearns traders.

The latter part of the book will address options for preventing similar disasters from recurring and will provide readers with practical guidelines for protecting themselves and their companies from various forms of fraud that were found to have played a role in the current economic and financial crisis.

Let it be noted at the outset that American economic and financial history is blemished with numerous catastrophic events, the most devastating of which was, of course, the Great Depression. The history lesson that needs to be kept in mind however, is that as much as our political leaders may try, they will never be able to safeguard America's financial institutions from future crises. It can only be hoped that with a thorough understanding of the factors and forces that triggered the crisis of 2007–2008, there is at least a chance that those who lead our nation will have the wisdom and foresight to render these future events far less painful than those the country endured beginning in the summer of 2007.

A note on terminology: Unlike the Great Depression, the financial crisis that is the subject of this book has not as yet been blessed with a colloquial household name. In the interest of simplicity and consistency, the crisis will generally be referred to in these pages as "the financial crisis of 2007–2008" or "the meltdown of 2007–2008" (the two years during which most of the damage and panic occurred).

Acknowledgments

M any of the people who offered valuable insight and perspective on key topics in this book insisted on anonymity in exchange for doing so. As part of the deal, they also required exclusion from this segment of the book. However, they know who they are and for their assistance I am indeed sincerely appreciative.

Thomas Scanlon, CPA, CFP, a seasoned accountant at Connecticut-based Borgida & Company, provided essential feedback throughout the book.

Stephen Pedneault, CFE, CPA, another Connecticut CPA and a razor-sharp antifraud expert, also helped by sharing his experiences and detailed knowledge of key types of fraud that played direct or indirect roles in the period leading up to the Great Crash.

Chris Doxey of Business Strategy, Inc. in Grand Rapids, Michigan was a great sounding board for many of the ideas that went into putting this book together. Chris has a unique view of the world of corporate crime, having been directly involved in developing antifraud controls at companies *after* they fell victim to financial trickery similar to that which came into play leading up to the 2007–2008 crisis.

Thanks also to Tim Burgard of John Wiley & Sons, along with his team of editors, whose efforts in forcing adherence to tight deadline schedules ensured that this volume appeared much earlier than it otherwise might have.

INTRODUCTION

A Brief History of Fraud in Financial Markets

The subprime mania that swept the home mortgage and securities markets, starting around 2002–2003, was the last straw for the U.S. financial system as we knew it since the early years of the twentieth century. Since the establishment of central banking in 1913, the American economy has toughed out several recessions. But never before 2007—including the devastating years of the Great Depression—has the economy and financial system come as close to utter obliteration.

It is no coincidence though that the financial services industry was the breeding ground for the deadly forces that brought on the Great Crash of 2008 and its aftershocks.

It is also no surprise that fraud played a starring role in the emergence of these dark chapters in American financial history. But it is important to understand the dynamics of earlier economic and financial crises in order to fully appreciate the genesis of the 2008–2009 meltdown and the key role that criminal activity played in it.

Banking Fraud in the Early Days

Before the Civil War, the United States had a banking and financial system that could be described as "sketchy" at best. Prior to the advent of the railroad, barons like Jay Gould and Cornelius Vanderbilt who exploited the underdeveloped and woefully mis-regulated businesses of borrowing and lending, made several failed attempts to create a central bank.

One of the federal government's efforts to establish a national bank resulted in what is believed to be the largest management-level bank fraud in post-Revolutionary history.

The target bank was the Second Bank of the United States (SBUS), an institution that was two years in the making thanks to intractable political divisiveness between supporters of state banking and those who favored national banking. When the SBUS was finally opened in early 1816, there were 19 branches, of which the Baltimore and Philadelphia branches were among the largest. Another nine were opened between 1817 and 1830.

The heads of these branches, along with other directors and executives, exploited the country's new frenzy over bank stocks and proceeded to purchase controlling shares in the SBUS. They used their power to establish their own financial firm whose sole mandate apparently was to manipulate SBUS stock. Specifically, one ploy used to drive up the price of SBUS shares was to pledge their previously purchased SBUS shares as collateral for loans from the SBUS in order to buy more of the bank's own shares. Though such unscrupulous activity would today be viewed as the worst possible form of insider trading, it went unpunished for several years within the SBUS. Worse, the bank executives cooked the bank's books to conceal these internal sham loans. But the scheme went unnoticed due to a "see-no-evil" mind-set among the bank's directors that sounds disturbingly similar to the mindset of the top bosses at Countrywide, Washington Mutual, and other major players in the subprime lending busi-ness of the early 2000s who chose to turn a blind eye to the rampant mortgage fraud that was making them mountains of money. (More on this in Chapter 5.)

Ultimately the SBUS conspirators were caught, but, curiously enough, a Congressional investigation into the fraud resulted in no recommendations for punitive action against the perpetrators, despite the findings of blatant violations of bank operating rules and laws.[1]

Following the failure of the SBUS, Washington made further efforts to stabilize the economy and monetary system. It did so by issuing currencies of numerous varieties from gold and silver coins to demand notes to United States Notes affectionately dubbed "greenbacks." Federal efforts to bring stability to the monetary system continued to be undermined by the cycle of issuance and retraction of state-issued currencies that continued over the decades leading up to the Civil War.

These were the products of "free banking" which is best described as minimally regulated state banking in which anyone could open a bank with next to no capital and issue its own banknotes (currency) as loans to customers. Unfortunately for most holders of these notes, the limited geographical usefulness of the currency inevitably resulted in drastic depreciation and ultimate losses.

While these monetary systems were loosely regulated by state governments and as such were not fraudulent in and of themselves, they did enable bank owners to exploit the system to illegal ends. They would purchase goods with the notes immediately after issuance and get out of Dodge. Due to inadequate backing by shareholder equity, the notes would quickly become worthless, the bank would fail, and the note holders would be left with nothing.[2]

On a more brazenly fraudulent level, free banking gave rise to what was aptly called wildcat banking. It took hold in numerous states, initially in Michigan and then in New York and several other states. According to one top economic historian, this is how it worked:

If the bond security [of the bank] was valued at more than its market value, individuals had an incentive to buy bonds, issue notes, and abscond with the proceeds.

For example, if someone could buy $80,000 worth of bonds at current market prices and the bonds were valued as security at their face value of, say, $100,000, and the notes could be passed for more than $80,000, say $90,000, there is a one-time gain of $10,000 in starting the bank. If the owner could avoid being sued for noteholders' losses, for example by leaving the court's jurisdiction, this difference between the amount received for the notes and the market value of the bonds created an incentive to start a bank and let it fail quickly.[3]

Along with wildcat banking came rampant counterfeiting and other swindles. Fortunately for the average American, the free banking system was shut down by the federal government through a levying of debilitating taxes. The banking industry then became a federally-run system, with a whole new set of flaws and regulatory loopholes.

This ongoing state of financial dysfunction brought with it some relatively complex financial frauds, highlighted in 1867 by the landmark collapse of Credit Mobilier, a construction company-turned-financial institution indirectly owned by the financial promoters of the Union Pacific Railroad, which was itself controlled by the federal government at the time.

The bank, originally organized by the aptly named George Francis Train, existed for the prime purpose of financing the railroad's construction in exchange for ample "returns" generated by drawing down substantial loans that the government had earlier provided to the railroad. But shortly after Congressman Oake Ames took over the "bank," it was learned that Ames had generously spread Credit Mobilier shares among numerous Congressional colleagues to secure votes on additional federal funding that was purportedly needed to complete the railroad's construction. The first major incident of pre-nineteenth century financial fraud made the history books when the loan's proceeds, to the tune of $23 million, ended up in the Credit Mobilier owners' pockets.

The subsequent collapse of Credit Mobilier thus also earned the dubious distinction as the first major American financial institution failure. The event shed light on America's woefully underdeveloped financial and regulatory structure.

Paradoxically, this period—the latter half of the nineteenth century, which Mark Twain dubbed "The Gilded Age" in an 1873 eponymous novel he co-authored with Charles Warner—was a time of unprecedented industrial advancement and rapid population growth. It was the period during which the oil empire of John D. Rockefeller was built; when Andrew Carnegie joined the elite ranks of the super-rich by master-crafting the largest steel company in America; and when modern industrial infrastructure including railroads, steel, and utilities took root.

Market-Building by Morgan

During this period, in 1892–1893, the first "real" stock market crash occurred, as well as the era of the "Money Trust" of the early 1890s—a term that came to be synonymous with John Pierpont Morgan.[4]

Through the turn of the century and into the 1920s, Morgan built his father Junius's London-based business partnership with American banker extraordinaire, George Peabody into the United States' first major investment banking firm. During those years, Morgan managed to earn a reputation of what former banking executive and financial historian, Charles Morris defined as "absolute integrity and straight dealing."[5]

Morgan was the builder of modern securities markets, replacing the one-stop pseudo-monopolistic financing approach of Jay Gould. Under Morgan, *shareholders* actually became living, breathing investors to be respected and reckoned with.

He accomplished this by recapitalizing the railroads with fresh cash, much of it originating in Europe where, in part thanks to his father's accomplishments, Morgan commanded enormous admiration and respect. He simplified the capital structure of the railroads into no more than two layers of debt with interest rates that the railroads' cash flows could comfortably manage. Equity meanwhile was sold to a broad market of investors.

And then came The Great War, which sparked a massive appetite for credit on the part of the Allies. Almost overnight the dollar became the "modernized" world's leading currency. To raise funds for their war efforts, France and Britain turned to JP Morgan for help. In what was at the time the largest bond issuance ever, the Morgan dynasty orchestrated a $500 million debt offer, cleverly selling them as "trade finance" bonds instead of what they really were—"war bonds."[6]

By the time the United States entered the war—in 1917—demand for U.S.-issued bonds was so great that the U.S. Treasury was able to successfully market some $17 billion of its own debt in the final year or so of the war.

By war's end, so many "average" Americans had bought government debt that demand for consumer investment services was more than adequate to fuel the rapid emergence of the country's retail securities industry.

Flim Flam Finance

Unsurprisingly, with the rapid growth of Western capitalism in the late-nineteenth and early-twentieth centuries came great temptation for employees *and* outsiders to steal from the country's rapidly increasing number of banks and investment houses. But in the end it was naive individual would-be investors who suffered most at the hands of swindlers peddling bogus securities to a public delirious with visions of overnight riches.

Things got progressively more precarious throughout the "Roaring 1920s" which saw the frenzy over government debt spread to equities and residential real estate. And while only about two million Americans actually owned stock by the time the market crashed in October 1929, the spread of securities holdings among American investors was substantial enough to give rise to a greatly exaggerated appreciation of the impact of the market dive than was actually justified. In fact, as many historians have written, the market crash was *not* the cause of the Great Depression. Rather, it was a by-product of misguided monetary policy and colossally misconceived foreign trade policy in the form of the Smoot-Hawley Act of 1930 which effectively choked off imports through astronomical tariffs, thus triggering inflation and sluggish economic growth in Europe which had been the source of large amounts of needed investment capital in the fast-growing U.S. manufacturing base.

It is nonetheless undeniable that the spirit of speculation that gripped the U.S. stock market beginning in the mid-1920s had "imminent disaster" written all over it. And, not entirely unlike the events of 2007–2008, fraud played a major role in bringing on the inevitable bursting of the bubble. Huge amounts of bogus stock were sold to investors, rich and poor, while legitimate issues of equities experienced stupendous price growth within very short periods of time.

One of the more colorful examples of this financial chaos is the story of Ivar Kreuger, a Swedish entrepreneur who built his father's tiny match manufacturing business into the world's dominant supplier of "safety matches."

Kreuger arrived in the United States in 1922 having realized that the poverty of many European governments after World War I provided an opportunity for capitalists with cash. He arranged for large loans—up to $125 million—to governments in return for official match monopolies. The scheme worked so well that, by 1930, Krueger controlled 90 percent of the world's match production.

But Kreuger was a fraud, a Bernard Madoff–type Ponzi schemer. His was by some accounts the largest financial fraud to date in U.S. history. He told prospective American investors that the foreign loans whose bonds he was peddling were risk-free since they were secured by an excise tax on match sales—the proceeds of which went into a trust account at a Kreuger-owned bank until the loan and interest were paid.

According to one account:

The source of Kreuger's capital was the American public. Since his company's securities were often issued in small denominations, many of Kreuger's stocks and bonds ended up in the hands of small investors. For instance, Kreuger issued $5 bonds, whereas the minimum at other corporations was $1,000. Kreuger's securities, both bonds and the stocks of his many subsidiaries, paid high returns to investors, yielding up to 20% annually on both stocks and (participating) bonds. Unfortunately, those dividends were largely paid out of capital, not profits. Because profits weren't substantial enough to pay the promised double-digit returns to bond investors, Kreuger's pyramid scheme ultimately collapsed.

The Depression accelerated the collapse of the Kreuger pyramid. Investors had little money to invest, and when there were no new investors there could be no dividend payments. Seeing the end of his empire and being hounded by an Ernst & Ernst auditor working for a legitimate subsidiary, Kreuger took his own life in Paris on March 12, 1932.

Initially, the world mourned his loss, but the truth was uncovered by Price Waterhouse auditors who were hired to unravel his affairs. Nearly a quarter of a billion dollars in assets apparently never existed. On the Monday following Kreuger's death, his securities accounted for 1/3 of the New York Stock Exchange volume, and lost 2/3 of their value. Within weeks the securities were worthless.[7]

Significantly, Kreuger's U.S. company had neither external nor internal auditors. Kreuger evidently saw no need for accurate financial records and hence there was no need for auditors. He insisted on strict secrecy about the financial condition of his company. This turned out to have been essential to the perpetration of his financial scheme since as noted above, once he was no longer in the picture, auditors discovered that he had been perpetrating a massive pyramid scheme, paying dividends to investors with capital from the company and investment income from new investors (sounds of Madoff?).

The generally unknown result of the Kreuger scandal was that it led to new federal laws, including perhaps most importantly, mandatory audits for listed companies, and other changes at the New York Stock Exchange.

As with the 2007–2008 bubble burst, in the crash of 1929 a panoply of egregious frauds helped to accelerate the country's slide toward disaster.

According to the records of an aggressive investigation into the stock market crash and its aftermath by a subcommittee of the Senate Committee on Banking and Currency, led by a Senate staffer, Ferdinand Pecora between 1932 and 1934, major banks, investments houses, and even law firms had peddled hundreds of millions of dollars of worthless stock leading up to the fateful day in October of 1929.

The Pecora Commission methodically dissected—and exposed—the malodorous actions of virtually every "big-name" Wall Street firm, including Chase National Bank, J.P. Morgan & Co., Kuhn Loeb and Co., National City Bank, and its so-called "securities affiliate," National City Co.

The latter two names are of particular interest in that according to the Pecora Commission, one of the most brazen frauds of the 1920s was perpetrated by the large New York banks flogging off massive amounts of worthless securities to their securities "affiliates," thereby applying copious layers of financial cosmetics to their own balance sheets.

And in yet another incident eerily similar to the self-enriching conduct of the captains of Lehman Brothers, Merrill Lynch, and other sinking Wall Street super ships in late 2008, Ferdinand Pecora uncovered the fact that while the market was crashing in 1929, Chase's then-boss, Albert Wiggin, made a $4 million profit as his bank's stock price rapidly tanked.[8]

In the end, the important but little-known fact is that the Pecora Commission's work to expose the criminal activities of financial institutions in the late 1920s led directly to the drafting and ultimate passage of the Securities Act of 1933, the Securities Exchange Act of 1934, and the Glass-Steagall Act of 1933.

Savings and Loan Fraud Follies

Beginning in the early 1980s, Congress lifted a number of key regulations that were stifling savings and loan institutions's ability to attract deposits and make profitable home loans. But within a few short years, the pendulum had swung to a climate of virtually complete deregulation which immediately attracted a band of non-banker investors who smelled an opportunity for easy riches with minimum financial risk. So unfettered were these new S&L owners in how they managed their operations, that they ended up with billions of dollars worth of ultra-high risk real estate loans on their books—many designed to benefit the owners themselves through arrangements that would today be characterized as unadulterated self-dealing. Simultaneously they feasted on the inflow of depositors' savings to pay for lavish lifestyles—often with brazen disregard for criminal laws prohibiting the misuse of depositor funds.

Of course as their Wild West banking practices ultimately produced wave after wave of defaults, the entire industry imploded and the federal government was left to clean up the mess and prosecute some of the most offensive scoundrels such as Charles Keating, Don Dixon, and others who ultimately did hard time for looting hundreds of millions of depositor dollars, brazen book cooking, and other serious financial felonies.

Beginning of the End

As the S&L crisis was winding down, the subprime mortgage industry was just shedding its training wheels. In 1990, there was effectively no secondary market for loans that were not "conforming"—that is, loans that didn't meet the credit standards of Fannie Mae and its companion government sponsored enterprise (GSE), Freddie Mac. These were mortgage loans up to $417,000 for a single family home whose borrower(s) had specified credit scores and income levels considered by the GSEs' policymakers to be "adequate" to make the loan affordable.

In 1999, a total of $2.9 trillion in mortgage-backed securities (MBS) and collateralized debt obligations (CDO) were on the books of the government "agencies"—mainly Fannie Mae and Freddie Mac. By the end of 2007, that amount had ballooned to $6 trillion.[9]

The modern-day makings of the worst crisis since the Great Depression started taking root in 1983 when the Federal National Mortgage Association Fannie Mae—the federal home mortgage giant—issued the first-ever collateralized mortgage obligation (CMO). These were securities that "elaborated" on the first securitized products—MBSs, which were the brainchild of a Salomon Brothers' trader named Lew Ranieri.[10]

One of the clearest descriptions of these financial "products"—which in subsequent years gave rise to mind-numbingly complex offshoots—was offered by Cameron L. Cowen, a partner at the New York City law firm, Orrick, Herrington, and Sutcliffe, in testimony given in late 2003 to the House Subcommittee on Housing and Community Opportunity and the House Subcommittee on Financial Institutions and Consumer Credit:

> *CMOs redirect the cash flows of trusts to create securities with several different payment features. The central goal with CMOs was to address prepayment risk—the main obstacle to expanding demand for mortgage backed securities, (MBS). Prepayment risk for [basic] MBS investors is the unexpected return of principal stemming from consumers who refinance the mortgages that back the securities. Homeowners are more likely to refinance mortgages when interest rates are falling. As this translates into prepayment of MBS principal, investors are often forced to reinvest the returned principal at a lower return. CMOs accommodate the preference of investors to lower prepayment risk with classes of securities that offer principal repayment at varying speeds. The different bond classes are also called tranches (a French word meaning slice). Some tranches—CMOs can include 50 or more—can also be subordinate to other tranches. In the event loans in the underlying securitization pool default, investors in the subordinate tranche would have to absorb the loss first.*
>
> *As part of the Tax Reform Act of 1986, Congress created the Real Estate Mortgage Investment Conduit (REMIC) to facilitate the issuance of CMOs. Today almost all CMOs are issued in the form of REMICs. In addition to varying maturities, REMICs can be issued with different risk*

characteristics. REMIC investors—in exchange for a higher coupon payment—can choose to take on greater credit risk. Along with a simplified tax treatment, these changes made the REMIC structure an indispensable feature of the MBS market. [In 2003,] Fannie Mae and Freddie Mac [were] the largest issuers of this security.

Asset-Backed Securities

The first asset-backed securities (ABS) date to 1985 when the Sperry Lease Finance Corporation created securities backed by its computer equipment leases. Leases, similar to loans, involve predictable cash flows. In the case of Sperry, the cash flow comes from payments made by the lessee. Sperry sold its rights to the lease payments to an off-book legal entity called a Special Purpose Vehicle (SPV). Interests in the SPV were, in turn, sold to investors through an underwriter.[11]

As Cowen went on to explain to the Subcommittees, the ABS market quickly grew as Wall Street started securitizing and marketing debt related to and including auto loans, credit card receivables, home equity loans, manufactured housing loans, student loans, and even future entertainment royalties.

According to Paul Muolo and Mathew Padilla, in their co-authored book, *Chain of Blame*, the initial motor behind CMOs was Larry Fink, head of mortgage trading at the investment firm, First Boston (absorbed in 1988 by Credit Suisse), who came up with the idea of creating a trust that guaranteed payments to the bondholders.[12]

There was nothing unethical, illegal, or even particularly risky about these securities in their early years. But, as upcoming chapters will reveal, these and their offspring which came to be defined by the catch-all term, "derivatives," spawned trading and sales tactics that in many cases were anything but above-board.

Off to the Races

The subprime mortgage industry, which originated a paltry $35 billion in 1995 swelled to $190 billion in 2001 and to $600 billion in 2006.

Similarly, between 2001 and 2006, the number of mortgage brokers exploded from an estimated 37,000 to some 53,000.

The beginning of the end for the subprime mortgage business—and for financial stability as we knew it—came when in the mid-1990s, Lehman Brothers became the first major investment bank to, in the words of former subprime mortgage lender Richard Bitner, "aggressively enter the business."[13]

Given the circumstances of its 2008 demise, it is in retrospect unsurprising that Lehman's 1990's foray into subprime territory proved disastrous. The event represents what is believed to be the first instance of Wall Street–related subprime mortgage fraud. In Bitner's words:

In 1995, when [Lehman] provided financing for First Alliance Mortgage Co. and underwrote the securities, Lehman's own internal memos questioned whether some borrowers had the capacity for repayment. As other investment banks backed away from First Alliance, federal and state regulators started to investigate their practices. Throughout the turmoil, Lehman continued to support First Alliance, keeping the operation in business. . . .

In 1993 a California jury awarded over $50 million in damages against First Alliance and attributed 10 percent of the responsibility to Lehman's involvement. It was eventually discovered that many of the sales tactics used by loan officers at First Alliance confused and misled borrowers.[14]

Lehman also settled a lawsuit filed in Broward County Circuit Court by Florida authorities who charged Lehman with being an "accomplice" in First Alliance's frauds. While admitting no wrongdoing, Lehman agreed to pay $400,000 and "review its practices."[15]

In true super-aggressive Lehman form, the firm also entered into a joint venture with Amresco, Inc., a struggling Dallas-based publicly traded subprime firm that thus became the first Wall Street firm to operate an actual subprime lending unit. It was called Finance America.

Chapters 5 and 6 will address the morbid details of how this rather inelegant birth of the subprime mortgage industry progressed to a period of relative financial sanity to one of questionable activity and ultimately to one effectively defined by one direct player as an "industry" of "fraud factories" which ultimately brought it crashing down.

It is important to keep in mind that the subprime crisis, besmirched as it was by rampant fraud, was not *solely* responsible for bringing the U.S. financial system to the brink.

Other critical factors include:

- Misguided or nonexistent regulation of banking and investment firm activity
- The unprecedented intensity of global competition in financial markets
- A partial failure to remedy the wounds to America's reputation as the financial standard bearer of the world after the rash of mega-corporate scandals of the early 2000s
- A management culture in financial services firms of indifference and denial with regard to the growing problem of fraud within their ranks

From the preceding pages, it is clear that the meltdown of 2007–2008 was not an isolated incident. However, it will ultimately be recorded as one of the worst financial crises in the country's colorful history of financial calamities, each of which is to varying degrees attributable to what over the decades has arguably become a culturally ingrained propensity for fraud throughout the financial industry.

Each of these powerful forces will be addressed in detail in upcoming chapters, with the objective of creating a complete perspective of the sometimes complex but invariably sobering impact of fraud on pushing the world's preeminent financial system to disaster on more than just a few occasions.

Notes

1. Edward S. Kaplan, *The Bank of the United States and the American Economy* (Santa Barbara, CA: Greenwood Publishing Group, 1999), 63.
2. Federal Reserve Bank of Atlanta, Gerald P. Dwyer Jr., "Wildcat Banking, Banking Panics, and Free Banking in the United States," *Economic Review*, December (1996): 6–7.
3. Federal Reserve Bank of Atlanta, Gerald P. Dwyer Jr., research by Hugh Rockoff, economist, cited in "Wildcat Banking, Banking Panics, and Free Banking in the United States," *Economic Review*, December (1996): 11.
4. Charles R. Morris, *Money, Greed, and Risk: Why Financial Crises and Crashes Happen* (New York: Times Books, 1999), 53.
5. Ibid., 53.
6. Ibid., 62.
7. Gaurav Kumar, Dale L. Flesher, and Tonya Flesher, *Ivar Kreuger Reborn: A Swedish/American Accounting Fraud Resurfaces in Italy and India*, available at SSRN: http://ssrn.com/abstract=1025525.
8. Jerry W. Markham, *A Financial History of the United States*, (Armonk, NY: M.E. Sharpe Inc., 2002), 1:146.
9. Securities Industry and Financial Markets Association (SIFMA). www.sifma.org.
10. Paul Muolo and Mathew Padilla, *Chain of Blame: How Wall Street Caused the Mortgage and Credit Crisis* (Hoboken, NJ: John Wiley & Sons, 2008), 56.

11. Statement of Cameron L. Cowan, Partner at Orrick, Herrington, and Sutcliffe LLP, on behalf of the American Securitization Forum before the Subcommittee on Housing and Community Opportunity, Subcommittee on Financial Institutions and Consumer Credit United States House of Representatives, Hearing on Protecting Homeowners, "Preventing Abusive Lending While Preserving Access to Credit," November 5, 2003.
12. Muolo and Padilla, *Chain of Blame*, 57.
13. Richard Bitner, *Confessions of a Subprime Mortgage Lender: An Insider's Tale of Greed, Fraud, and Ignorance* (Hoboken, NJ: John Wiley & Sons, 2008), 110.
14. Ibid.
15. Michael Hudson, "How Wall Street Stocked the Mortgage Meltdown," *Wall Street Journal Online*, June 28, 2007.

Fraud in the Markets

CHAPTER 1

The Fraud Culture

A merican organizations lose approximately 7 percent of gross revenue to fraud *every year*, according to the Association of Certified Fraud Examiners (ACFE).[1]

In 2006 (the last year for which data are available), of 21 industries studied by the ACFE, banking/financial services topped the list in terms of number of internal fraud incidents reported. A fairly distant second was the government and public administration, followed by healthcare.[2]

What does this tell us about fraud in the financial services industry? Other than the obvious fact that 7 percent of gross revenue of *any* bank or financial services firm represents a large sum of money, the industry's dubious distinction as having the most incidents of internal fraud speaks to the disturbing reality that fraudulent behavior has become integral to the culture of this sector.

The reasons for this are complex but it is hoped that understanding them will help political, industry, and social leaders come up with new laws and regulations to control the fraud problem in financial services.

As for professionals whose duties *include* fraud detection and prevention, understanding the mentality of this "fraud culture" is *essential* to developing deterrents, incentives,

1

regulations, laws, and any other potential weapons for effectively stopping the growth of this cancer.

Without knowing how and why the basic values and ethics of large swathes of the financial industry became egregiously compromised, there is little chance of restoring the integrity, fairness, and respect for others that—reassuringly—represent the ethical guidelines by which many financial executives and professionals still conduct their affairs.

I Wanna Be Rich

As the "Land of Opportunity," America has for over 200 years provided better odds of success than any economic system in history to individuals seeking to become materially wealthy. It is thus not surprising that America has always been the country with the largest number of ultra-wealthy individuals. In *Forbes* magazine's latest tally, 11 of the world's 25 richest people reside in the United States.

This is surely not a bad thing. Together with constitutionally guaranteed political, economic, and civil freedoms and a unique cultural spirit of optimism, ingenuity, and excellence, this "golden promise" has made America the most successful free market nation in history.

Similarly, the successes of America's first generation of true business icons like Morgan, Carnegie, and Rockefeller, and most recently, Gates, Buffett, Jobs, and Trump, have reinforced the inspiration of millions who choose to devote themselves to the pursuit of financial happiness.

Historically, for most entrepreneurs, getting rich has been a *healthy* obsession—one that has pushed them to strive for perfection, work as hard as it takes, and commit to never giving up despite the risks. Many possessing these personality traits have built successful businesses that collectively employ millions, generate billions in tax revenue, and comprise the 20 million-plus small businesses responsible for the lion's share of U.S. economic growth.

But the American promise of limitless wealth has long been tainted by a subculture of individuals possessed of the misconception that becoming wealthy is easy. These folks subscribe to the false notion that getting rich—preferably quickly—is a fundamental entitlement of every American citizen. What they fail to realize is that the entitlement bestowed by the Constitution is simply to *pursue* wealth—*not* to have it hand-delivered by the U.S. Department of Getting-Rich-Quick.

Many thus learn the hard way that getting rich—to put it bluntly—ain't easy. Many give up when they run up against this disheartening reality. Most find contentment in alternative pursuits and non-material achievements, such as raising a family, pursuing hobbies, involving themselves in community volunteer activities, and so on.

However, a small but by no means insignificant contingent of wealth-seekers *don't* give up, despite a lack of resourcefulness, reluctance to invest personal capital, and, most important of all, the absence of sufficient drive to put in the long hours and weather the inevitable stresses to get a successful wealth-generating enterprise off the ground.

These are the individuals who resort to cutting ethical and legal corners to achieve their financial goals. They are the ones whose collective misconduct results in the estimated $1 trillion in fraud losses sustained by U.S. organizations collectively *every year.*

It is to understanding the psychology, motives, and mentalities of these wrongdoers whose financial misconduct costs corporate America so dearly and has frayed the fabric of American social values since the 1970s, that this book is dedicated.

The Spread of Ethical Erosion

Since the early 1930s manifestations of what has been referred to as "white-collar crime" have been evident at varying levels of severity. Offenders range from the one-time embezzler who takes just enough from his or her employer to get through an isolated bad patch, to the criminally compulsive captains of industry who looted their companies or drove them to financial ruin. Also included are crimes by those whose professional status encompasses ranks superior to those of hourly laborers, which have all been amply chronicled.

Every one of them has had his or her own reasons for doing what they did. And every one of them has rationalized in one way or another their criminal conduct.

It is the uninterrupted spread of this culture of "justifiable corner cutting" that explains much of why the financial markets were driven to the brink of disaster in 2007 and 2008. It was an unbridled money grab which originated in the late 1970s when names like Michael Milken and Ivan Boesky jumped on to the front pages of American newspapers and gripped the nation from Wall Street to Main Street. The trend played out through a perfect storm of deadly forces including:

- The Wild West–like hawking by ethically-challenged brokers of too-good-to-be-true mortgages to borrowers who either were talked into believing—or truly did believe—that they could make payments that they clearly could not.
- An unprecedented nationwide spending spree financed by consumer credit whose issuers clogged mailboxes with little plastic rectangles dressed up as licenses to shop until you drop, but with so many hidden financial tripwires that the rate of default on credit cards inevitably rose to all-time highs.

- Wall Street's headlong foray into new high-risk securities called derivatives, so complex that even supposedly sophisticated Ivy League mathematicians could hardly comprehend them, but which the industry's army of marketing mavens managed to persuade pension funds, multinational corporations, global banks, and self-described investment geniuses to purchase by the billions.

- The explosion of mind-boggling technological "tools" mushrooming from the global envelopment of the Internet into cellular telecommunications, powerful financial and investment software, wireless computing connectivity, and high-volume electronic data management. All were developed by techno-wizards with laudable intentions, but were promptly adapted by what came to be known as the "black hat" community of high-tech fraudsters, saboteurs, and terrorists.

- A full-blown epidemic of cyber-driven identity theft and fraud that sandbagged the financial lives of tens of millions of Americans. Information security breaches such as those that victimized retail giant TJX, credit card processor Heartland, and even Microsoft and JP Morgan Chase resulted in billions in banking and retail losses and compromised the belief system of a nation of trusting consumers by eroding their faith in the banking system and raised their suspicions about on-line commerce, Internet banking, and other twenty-first century technological advances that could have, and *should* have, bolstered America's global competitiveness and economic well-being.

The product of these forces was a palpable erosion of America's value system of community, charity, and benevolence in favor of an "every-man-for-himself" mindset that has directly or indirectly fueled a boom in fraud of all kinds. The following statistics, after all, are not arbitrary. They reflect the confluence of the forces discussed above, as well as other factors that researchers have yet to understand:

- The 7 percent of gross revenue lost to internal fraud mentioned earlier currently represents nearly $1 trillion in fraud losses, not counting the additional billions lost to external fraud such as cyber-attacks, organized crime syndicates, and the exploits of dishonest vendors, ex-employees, and customers.[3]
- The Federal Trade Commission (FTC) reported that in 2008, 643,195 Americans filed complaints of having been victimized by fraudsters. That number represented a startling increase of nearly 50 percent from 428,394 in 2006.[4]
- The U.S. financial services industry experienced the largest number of internal fraud incidents of the 21 industries studied by the ACFE.
- The number of victims of identity theft skyrocketed between 2000 and 2009 from 31,100 to 1.2 million.[5]

What It All Means

Fraud and corruption have always been components of American culture. The Mob, Tammany Hall, Prohibition-related political graft, union corruption, securities fraud in the pre-Depression era, the Savings and Loan (S&L) fraud fiasco of the 1980s, corporate scandals like Enron, Tyco, WorldCom, and HealthSouth in the 1990s and 2000s, and now the subprime mortgage meltdown and related securities frauds like those that brought down Bear Stearns collectively portray an American cultural landscape with criminal blemishes aplenty.

However, as statistics and the personal experiences of many Americans over the age of 45 confirm, fraud, corruption, and ethical misconduct was *not* as prevalent in the 1970s and early 1980s as it is now.

Indeed the occasional corrupt city official, local judge, or state representative made headlines from time to time in earlier times. And of course the Mob's grip on the gaming industry made it a hotbed of financial skullduggery starting in the 1930s.

But the fraud-driven destruction of a $100 billion company like Enron? The theft of $65 billion through a one-man Ponzi scheme? The demise of a Wall Street icon like Bear Stearns at the hands of two rogue hedge fund managers? Such earth-shattering incidents were practically unheard of until the late 1980s.

Why? The late 1970s and early 1980s marked the early stages of what would become the perfect storm of the 2000s. It was the period of unmitigated financial abuse by a contingent of moral misfits who abused deregulation of the S&L industry to steal $150 billion of depositor and investor funds.

It was the period of Michael Milken whose junk bond exploits and insider trading crimes shook Wall Street and made him Public Enemy Number One in the financial world.

And it was the period of corporate raiding, dismantling, dissolving, and divesting. Not illegal or particularly unethical per se. But fuel for the demise of Wall Street decorum and collegiality and the ascent of personal avarice that some would say culminated in the financial crisis of 2007–2008, by which time long-standing written and unwritten rules of fair play among financial institutions had been discarded as so much ticker tape.

John Bogle, the revered founder and long-time CEO of the Vanguard Group of Mutual Funds, explains the change this way: "Unchecked market forces overwhelmed traditional standards of professional conduct, developed over centuries."

"The result is a shift from moral absolutism to moral relativism. We've moved from a society in which 'there are some things that one simply does not do' to one in which 'if everyone else is doing it, I can too.' Business ethics and professional standards were lost in the shuffle."[6]

Irony played no small role in this 30-plus-year saga. The baby boomers who made the Woodstock period a historical milestone in the same category as Lincoln's emancipation of the slaves and Kennedy's triumph in the Cuban Missile Crisis, were the generation of *anti-materialism*. They worshipped Vonnegut and Brecht and disdained two-car garages. They embraced diversity and selflessness and vilified the military industrial complex.

And where did they end up when they walked into the real world with their Ivy League diplomas and their promise to help build a "pseudo-socialistic, back-to-the-land" America?

Though Bill Clinton never inhaled, it is without doubt that many of his less self-disciplined contemporaries who did ultimately cut their hair, shed their bell-bottoms and landed on Wall Street, in the prestigious litigation departments of white-shoe Manhattan law firms and in the trenches of America's preeminent financial institutions that led the Western world to a new post-war period of unparalleled abundance, prosperity, and the promise of limitless fast-action material potential.

As John Talbott, a former Goldman Sachs investment-banker-turned-author wrote in one of his illuminating books, one of the driving forces of the 1990s housing boom was a "constant drive for status. Seeking status is a strong genetic urge.... It is hard to see the rationality of an American couple with fully grown children who had left home wanting to live in 12,000 square foot monster homes or own four and five cars. If not for status, that is."[7]

This mad dash for material excess was symptomatic of the money-grabbing culture mentioned above. It was intimately intertwined with the rationalizations by financial and corporate titans when they could not (or chose not to) resist the temptations to bend the rules, exploit regulatory loopholes, and commit the massive frauds that contributed to the explosive growth of white-collar crime in the 1990s and 2000s.

How We Got Here

It was of course the perplexingly intricate tapestry of stock markets, bond markets, derivatives markets, and virtual markets that became the feeding ground for technologically-driven money grabbers that took center stage in the "evolution" of American values in the latter decades of the twentieth century and into the first decade of the twenty-first.

In illustrating this multifaceted transfiguration, David Callahan, author of *The Cheating Culture*, points to the case of Scott Sullivan, the former CFO of WorldCom and right-hand man to the ill-fated company's CEO, Bernard Ebbers. Callahan notes that for a decade of his tenure at WorldCom, Sullivan lived with his wife in a modest home in South Florida that they bought in 1990 for $170,000. But between 1990 and 2000, when Sullivan's stake in WorldCom had peaked at more than $150 million, something profound changed in the CFO's psyche. "He [Sullivan] could have cashed out as an immensely wealthy man," writes Callahan. "He chose to stay on. And, over the next two years, WorldCom cooked its books with astonishing brazenness while Sullivan was CFO, the corporate official most directly responsible for the veracity of the company's numbers. WorldCom inflated its earnings by some $11 billion through a variety of financial manipulations. When the true accounting was completed by investigators, they alleged that Sullivan had directed the largest corporate fraud in history."

What caused this drastic abandonment of ethics and the embracing of a mindset which clearly lacked any moral compass whatsoever? As Callahan postulates, perhaps Sullivan viewed himself as a corporate hero, doing whatever was needed to preserve thousands of jobs. On the other hand, Callahan rightly points out that Sullivan had personal motives to fudge the numbers because his pay package was directly tied to the company's stock price.

Neither of these explanations, even if they actually co-existed, can possibly explain why a "normal" financial professional would turn so abruptly and unequivocally to financial crime. And herein lies the critical lesson of the Scott Sullivan tragedy (Sullivan spent five years in jail and lost all of his financial assets). Writes Callahan:

> *I believe that the best explanations of why we have more Scott Sullivans and Barry Bondses . . . boil down to changes in the economy and the new rules that govern it. Our winner-take-all system dangles immense rewards in front of people, bigger than ever before. And today's business culture demands, and glorifies, extreme levels of competitiveness. Meanwhile, the Winning Class has worked to emasculate government regulators . . . reshaping the rules so that it can get away with economic murder. . . . To understand the ethics of Scott Sullivan and his ilk, you have to understand how the values of American society have changed. . . . We have a nastier, more cutthroat set of values than previous generations did. As the race for money and status has intensified, it has become more acceptable for individuals to act opportunistically and dishonestly to get ahead. Notions of integrity have weakened. More of us are willing to make the wrong choices, at least when it comes to money and career.*[8]

The Evolving Shapes of Fraud

While evidence of Callahan's sobering cultural portrait abounds in our everyday lives—just turn on your local TV news anytime of the day or night—it begs the question: *How did we get this way?* To answer that, we must first understand *who* commits fraud.

There is some disparity in the findings of several research studies on how much of total fraud is committed by insiders compared with external perpetrators. Some data put the ratio at 60–40[9]; others come in closer to 80–20. In any case, most research shows that on average, the majority of fraud committed against *all* U.S. organizations is internal.

Who Are the Bad Guys?

Nonetheless, when it comes to external fraudsters, organizations have a dizzying array of perpetrators to worry about.

Most serious, in terms of the dollars involved (though not necessarily dollars *lost*), are money launderers. This group includes the far-flung global population of drug-traffickers, as well as members of organized crime, illegal gambling operators, and others.

Although financial institutions are directly responsible for monitoring and reporting money laundering activity, because they are typically not *parties* to such activity, they are not always *victims* of these crimes. Moreover, money laundering, while ranked by researchers as one of the largest "industries" in the world in terms of dollars transacted, has been around for centuries and as such does not require special analysis in the context of the financial crisis.

However, there are plenty of external fraudsters besides money launderers who cause massive losses to organizations of all kinds—and who thereby contribute to the cheating culture that David Callahan so accurately describes. Among these folks are:

- Dishonest customers (retail *and* commercial)
- Identity thieves/fraudsters
- Check forgers and counterfeiters
- Dishonest vendors

- Ex-employees
- Internet fraudsters (including phishing attackers, hackers, malicious code programmers)
- Credit card fraudsters
- Crooked mortgage brokers, lenders, appraisers, and attorneys.

Unfortunately, because external fraudsters are so varied in terms of the business, social, and geographical environments in which they operate, it is extremely difficult to identify common personal, behavioral, or demographic characteristics. They can be:

- Hardened career criminals
- Occasional opportunists
- People who target organizations for the "thrill of it"
- Individuals who do what they do out of desperation (which is increasingly the case during economic downturns, when, for example, banks regularly experience spikes in credit card fraud, identity-related frauds, and Internet crime)

The bottom line is that there are few if any behavioral or demographic characteristics common to all external fraudsters. However, we can safely say that their numbers are increasing, the financial damage they cause is growing, and the cultural degradation they perpetuate is definitive. Further detail on these outsider miscreants will be provided in Chapter 4.

The Insider Threat

Fortunately for fraud-fighters, *employees* who commit fraud do have common personality and behavioral traits. They are also prone to scientifically-proven psychological influences that help fraud prevention experts to identify them.

In general, research on internal fraud shows that about 80 percent of employees in any financial services institution are fundamentally honest.

If that is the case, you may wonder, how can internal fraud be such a costly threat to business, society, and American culture? Many fraud prevention experts use the so-called "20-60-20" rule to illustrate the human component of internal fraud:

- 20 percent of the people in any organization will never steal—no matter what. They are individuals whose character and integrity are so unwavering that nothing could pressure or tempt them to do anything dishonest.
- 60 percent of the people in the organization are "fence sitters." They are basically honest people. But, if given the *opportunity* to commit fraud and the risk is perceived to be minimal, they might cross the line.
- The remaining 20 percent are inherently dishonest. They will always commit fraud when the opportunity arises. In fact they will often *create* opportunities to steal or deceive if they think it will result in personal financial gain.[10]

To understand the insider fraud threat it is helpful to divide it into two key categories:

1. *Employee-level fraud.* This type of fraud is committed by people who are neither supervisors nor managers or executives. They may be salaried professionals or hourly employees.
2. *Management-level fraud.* These crimes are committed by managers at all levels—including the most senior levels. Many of the frauds committed by these individuals are the same as those committed by employees lower down the organization chart.

   Though committed with less frequency than employee-level fraud, virtually *all* management level frauds result in much greater losses than those perpetrated at lower levels.

This fact is underscored every time we hear about another senior executive being arrested, indicted, or convicted of a serious financial crime such as cooking the company's books, looting the business, or paying bribes.

The reason is clear: Managers have more authority and therefore more opportunity to cheat than those who work under them.

The Fraud Triangle

One set of factors common to internal fraudsters *at all levels in any organization* is the Fraud Triangle. The theory behind the Fraud Triangle was developed in the 1940s by a leading criminologist, Donald Cressey who conducted extensive research with convicted embezzlers to determine what motivated seemingly honest people to commit fraud.

His research led him to the conclusion that people who are experiencing severe financial problems about which they are embarrassed (or for other reasons cannot discuss with others), find ways to commit fraud—thinking that they won't get caught while convincing themselves that they are doing nothing wrong.

Eventually, Cressey's findings came to be summed up in what is now widely referred to in the antifraud profession as the "Fraud Triangle." Its three components—just as Cressey suggests in more complex wording—Pressure, Opportunity, and Rationalization (see Exhibit 1.1).

1. *Pressure* in the context of Cressey's Fraud Triangle relates specifically to financial difficulties such as large amounts of credit card debt, an overwhelming burden of unpaid healthcare bills, large gambling debts, extended unemployment, or similar financial difficulties.

EXHIBIT 1.1 Fraud Triangle

In the context of the financial crisis, such pressure manifested itself in cutthroat competitiveness and intensifying urgency to generate larger and larger profits.

2. *Opportunity* exists when an employee discovers a weakness in the organization's antifraud controls. Such a weakness might exist, for example, if an employee is able to set up a phony vendor and have fraudulent invoices paid and mailed to an address that he or she controls or if poor controls enable a senior bank executive to approve mortgages or other loans he knows to be fraudulent.

3. *Rationalization* is a psychological process whereby a person who has committed fraud convinces himself that the act is either not wrong, or that even though it *may* be wrong, it will be "corrected" because he will eventually return the money. At a much riskier level, such as that which prevailed in financial markets in the years leading up to the financial crisis, rationalization can involve self-justification of acts that may prove either calamitous, illegal, or both because the potential payoff is too great to ignore.

In essence, Cressey's theory teaches that when all three of these elements are in place in an individual's life, he or she is very likely to commit fraud (or already has). However, criminal justice experts and psychologists who have conducted research since the publication of Cressey's work argue persuasively that all three elements do *not* have to be in place for an individual to be driven to commit fraud. Indeed, there are numerous cases suggesting that financial pressure alone is enough to push an individual to *seek* an opportunity to steal and that rationalization played little if any role in premeditation of the crime.

Pressure, Opportunity, and Rationalization on Wall Street

Pressure

It is important to note that the Fraud Triangle's element of *pressure* can take many forms at both the executive and employee levels of financial institutions.

For example, exorbitant executive compensation packages took center stage in the debate over whether and how much federal bailout money should be handed out to the likes of Merrill Lynch, Citigroup, American International Group (AIG), and JPMorgan Chase. Many analysts, politicians, and pundits argued that the pressure on these executives to boost their companies' financial performance in order to "earn" bigger bonuses caused them to cut legal and ethical corners.

Though this issue is complex, there is little dispute that the resulting "culture" of short-term earnings performance that swept not only through the financial services industry but through American businesses in general in the 1990s and early 2000s did induce many top executives to cook the books in order to fatten their bonuses, or in some cases, to preserve their jobs.

To succeed, these bosses sought—and all too often found—*opportunities* to break the rules governing accounting and security matters in order to obtain the performance goals they felt pressured to attain.

Pressure at Lehman Brothers: An Extreme Example

In the wake of the implosion of the 160-year-old investment firm he had run for 15 years, Lehman Brothers' last CEO, Richard Fuld told Congress that he never regretted any of the decisions he had made in his final months at Lehman.

Fuld, who has been characterized by numerous Wall Street experts as ferociously competitive and dead-set on victory in every business challenge he takes on, proved to have exercised excessive hubris during the heyday of the subprime mortgage frenzy.

"He exuded hostility," said New York author and critic, Ken Auletta in an interview with ABC News.[11]

That quality apparently served him well over the 40 years he was employed by Lehman. But in his final years as CEO, Lehman amassed a reported $650 billion in assets, of which much was represented by risky subprime mortgage-backed securities, with only 3 percent in shareholder equity. This earned Fuld widespread criticism for having made over-the-top bets with far too much borrowed money.

No doubt, had Fuld read the tea leaves accurately and continued to grow the firm's profits as he had done by astounding leaps during his 15 years at the helm, he would have been the hero of Wall Street that he no doubt dreamed of becoming.

Lesson learned: Pressure, be it self-imposed or a product of the financial services "culture," drove some of the best and the brightest of Wall Street to take risks that would have been unheard of a short 10 years earlier. Their actions poured tankloads of fuel on the financial wildfire that threw the entire global financial system into a state of unprecedented panic and distress.

As illustrated in detail in Chapter 7, Richard Fuld was the archetypical tragic figure in this calamity.

Importantly, the Lehman Brothers implosion is not the only indicator of how the ego-driven, winner-take-all mentality that consumed Wall Street played a decisive role in hastening the onset of the financial crisis. Another high profile example is what took place with AIG. The insurance giant's problems began when four former executives of Berkshire Hathaway subsidiary, General Re, and one from former General Re client, AIG, were convicted on charges related to fraudulent financial transactions between the two insurance giants. In early 2008, a federal jury found them guilty on all 16 counts in their indictment, including conspiracy, securities fraud, mail fraud, and making false statements.

Specifically, prosecutors had accused the executives of inflating AIG's reserves by $500 million in 2000 and 2001 through fraudulent reinsurance deals that made AIG—General Re's largest client—look stronger than it was, thereby artificially boosting its stock price.

At the trial, former AIG Chief Executive Maurice R. ("Hank") Greenberg, who led the company for nearly four decades and is credited with most of its growth, and General Re's then chief executive, Joseph Brandon, were identified as unindicted co-conspirators.

The General Re frauds were perpetrated because the five executives felt pressure to embellish AIG's financials. The result was stiff prison sentences for the offenders. That Greenberg escaped conviction and punishment is a testament to his immense influence on Wall Street and in political circles. As an executive, however, he is no angel, according to numerous people who have had dealings with him, including one former senior executive who worked closely with him for many years. According to this person, who insisted on anonymity, Greenberg ran AIG with an iron fist and intimidated many a subordinate without restraint.

For his part, though, the pressure that Greenberg felt during this time was driven by his enormous ego. His primary mission in life, the former executive explained, was to ensure that AIG remained the largest insurance company in the world—*not* to amass more money for himself.

The key lesson within the context of the ominous attitudinal changes that took place in boardrooms in the 1990s and 2000s is that the Fuld and Greenberg examples are representative of an all too common ego-driven psychology of the ends justifying the means. It is not dissimilar from the mentality that pushed numerous other executives, including WorldCom's Bernard Ebbers, Adelphia's Rigas family, Tyco's Dennis Kozlowski and former Countrywide CEO, Angelo Mozilo, to be investigated and charged with serious financial crimes.

Opportunity

The internal controls *and regulatory oversight* that might have prevented many of the high-profile frauds of the 1990s were clearly absent. The well-documented string of financial reporting frauds beginning with Enron prompted Congress to ultimately pass the Sarbanes-Oxley Act (SOX) in 2002. Unfortunately, the events of subsequent years indicate that SOX has fallen short of its intended goal of eliminating many of the opportunities in large corporations to commit financial fraud.

In the securities world, for example, such opportunities often exist when employees are able to trade without adequate supervision or controls and can execute transactions for their own benefit. While, as mentioned earlier, this is not an uncommon occurrence, this trap was dramatically spotlighted in early 2008 when "rogue" trader, Jerome Kerviel of Société Générale was found to have lost the bank $7 billion by taking a number of large, unauthorized, but highly risky trading positions.

At middle management levels, poor controls or lack of oversight can enable dishonest insiders to:

- Falsify loan applications and other financial documents
- Authorize and/or approve phony appraisals of property for which financing is sought
- Collude with dishonest mortgage brokers

However, the "big-time," headline-grabbing financial institution frauds are those committed by top executives. In the context of *opportunity*, these crimes typically involve falsifying financial statements and records—in response to the pressure discussed above.

Opportunities to commit these potentially costly financial crimes exist when there is a lack of board oversight, weak internal controls over financial reporting, or when transactions of dubious legality are so complex that they cannot be readily understood let alone stopped before being carried out.

Rationalization

With regard to rationalization, the most common psychological justification for committing fraud at the top levels of financial services companies is, in crude terms, "whatever it takes."

Richard Girgenti, National Leader for KPMG's Forensic Practice used this exact term to describe the mindset that in recent years has overtaken U.S. businesses as a result of misguided performance reward systems. He added that "Restoring trust and confidence in the integrity of our capital markets and institutions will require business leaders to build corporate cultures that reward 'doing the right thing,'"[12] implying that the ethical culture of U.S. businesses has been strongly compromised by the pressures that "give rise to fraud risks."[13]

Although there is no scientific or academic research to explain the rise of the *rationalizing* attitude of "whatever it takes," the timeline appears consistent with the steady fragmentation of the financial services industry.

Recent history bears out Girgenti's assessment. Whereas Wall Street firms and banks throughout America (excluding perhaps S&Ls) had acquired an image of integrity, financial conservatism, stability, and unshakeable profitability in the early decades of the post–World War II era, this all came apart once the steamroller of acquisitions, mergers, and divestitures that populated the business news headlines shifted into high gear in the late 1980s, 1990s, and early 2000s.

The list of such acquisitions, mergers, and divestitures is lengthy. A helpful snapshot comprises the following milestones:

- Lehman sold itself in 1984 to Shearson, an American Express-backed electronic transaction company. Later the same year, the combined firms became Shearson Lehman/American Express.
- In 1988, Shearson Lehman/American Express and E.F. Hutton & Co. merged as Shearson Lehman Hutton Inc.
- In 1993, under newly appointed CEO, Harvey Golub, American Express began to divest itself of its banking and brokerage operations. It sold its retail brokerage and asset management operations to Primerica and in 1994 it spun off Lehman Brothers Kuhn Loeb in an initial public offering, as Lehman Brothers Holdings, Inc.
- Citicorp merged with Travelers Insurance in 1998. (The previous year, Travelers had absorbed Salomon Smith Barney). In 2001, Citi bought European-American Bank.

- In 2002, Citi acquired Golden State Bancorp, parent company of First Nationwide Mortgage and Cal Fed, the second-largest U.S. thrift.
- Between 2002 and 2005, Citi spun off Travelers.

The result: These and scores of other takeovers, mergers, divestitures, and partnerships between and among Wall Street firms essentially eradicated employee, management, and executive loyalty to any given institution. Replacing the "old school" purposefulness of long-term business builders such as John Reed of Citibank, Harvey Golub of American Express, Sanford Weill of Citicorp, and even Richard Fuld of Lehman Brothers, was a new brigade of short-term "money tacticians" who seemed to care little about the prestige, financial soundness, and long-term success of their employers. The only thing that motivated them was making money—any way they could.

In the late 1990s and early 2000s, the likes of Stan O'Neal of Merrill Lynch, Anthony Mozilo of Countrywide, and Kerry Killinger of Washington Mutual set the stage for a new way of doing business in the financial markets; one defined by a credo of "take no prisoners."

The mentality that governed the way subprime home mortgages were underwritten and approved in the years leading up to the financial crisis encapsulates this myopic "make-the-numbers" driver of pre-crisis financial services management.

This mindset was rather astoundingly summed up by James LaLiberte, former Chief Operating Officer People's Choice Bank a California-based subprime lender which filed for bankruptcy protection in 2007 and court-administered liquidation in 2008. LaLiberte told NBC News that People's Choice's chief appraiser had commented to him that "Fraud is what we do," referring to the bank's reported practice of approving loans based on fictitious home appraisals as well as egregiously falsified mortgage applications.

People's Choice is thus a perfect example of how mortgage lending became a vast playground for unscrupulous loan brokers, lenders, appraisers, underwriters, and executives. Another People's Choice employee—an underwriter—told NBC News that she was actually bribed by loan salespeople with cars, cash, and even breast implants in exchange for approving loan applications that were clearly doctored and were for borrowers who had no way of making the loan payments. (She said she declined these offers).

Unsurprisingly, People's Choice's founder and former CEO, Neil Kornsweit denied any knowledge of such nefarious activity, but such was the position of hundreds of top executives of failed or struggling subprime lenders who at least tacitly sanctioned out-of-control sales conduct by loan officers, appraisers, and underwriters.

A Triangle or a Diamond?

In recent years a few variations on the Fraud Triangle theory have emerged among antifraud professionals. They have been dubbed the "Fraud Diamond" or "Fraud Pentagon" due to the inclusion of additional psychological motives for employees to commit fraud.

In one interpretation of the evolution of a Fraud Diamond, the fourth part of the shape is closely related to rationalization. It occurs when an employee justifies committing a fraud by taking the attitude that he *deserves* the stolen money—because the company was unfair in denying him a raise or promotion, or that some other form of mistreatment made the individual a "victim."

Unfortunately, if we accept Callahan's argument that the cheating culture is well entrenched in America, we must also accept that the fourth element of the Fraud Diamond—employee disenfranchisement—will not be easy to counteract and that it will continue to gnaw at the ethical foundations of our culture.

This is especially so in light of the seemingly more important pressures—such as sustaining revenues and profits—that, as discussed earlier, weigh excessively on top decision makers. However, downplaying the importance of this management duty can result in costly fraud.

A Fraud Pentagon?

The People's Choice example, as well as the transformation of Wall Street from venerated standard bearer of international financial integrity to hotbed of numbers-chasing mayhem, provides background for a variation of the Fraud Diamond Theory discussed earlier.

It cannot be denied that in the period from 1999 until the onset of the financial crisis in mid-2007, unadorned lust for money became a root cause of the debacle.

The cycle fueled by Wall Street securitization of billions of dollars of fraudulently processed and default-prone loans which generated outlandish paydays for everyone from top Wall Street executives to Main Street subprime mortgage brokers spread a fog of avarice over the entire financial system, ultimately dooming it to its inevitable crash-and-burn.

The bottom line: By the mid-2000s, the Fraud Diamond, as it applied to the financial services industry, had morphed into a Fraud Pentagon with *personal greed* forming the fifth side of the shape and creating new characteristics and manifestations of the already deeply engrained fraud problem in the financial services industry.

In forthcoming chapters, we'll explore how all of this contributed substantially and directly to the eventual decline and collapse of the financial markets between 2006 and 2009 as well as how America fell from its lofty position of global financial superpower to the crippled welfare recipient of billions of federal bailout dollars.

Notes

1. Association of Certified Fraud Examiners (ACFE), *2008 Report to the Nation on Occupational Fraud and Abuse*, 8, www.acfe.com.
2. Ibid.
3. Ibid.
4. Federal Trade Commission, www.ftc.gov/bcp/edu/microsites/idtheft/.
5. Federal Trade Commission, Consumer Sentinel Network, www.ftc.gov/sentinel/reports/sentinel-annual-reports/sentinel-cy2008.pdf.
6. John Bogle, "A Crisis of Ethic Proportions," WSJ.com, April 20, 2009, http://online.wsj.com/article/SB124027114694536997.html.
7. John T. Talbott, *Contagion* (Hoboken, NJ: John Wiley & Sons, 2009), 39.
8. David Callahan, *The Cheating Culture: Why More Americans Are Doing Wrong to Get Ahead* (Orlando, FL: Harcourt Inc., 2004), 102–106.
9. PricewaterhouseCoopers, *Economic Crime: People, Culture and Controls. The 4th Biennial Global Economic Crime Survey* (2007), 8, www.pwc.com/gx/en/forms/gx-en-0380.jhtml.
10. Federal Bureau of Investigation, *Financial Institution Fraud and Failure Report*, 2005, www.fbi.gov/publications/financial/2005fif/fif05.pdf.
11. Alice Gomstyn, *Bleeding Green: The Fall of Fuld. Money, Respect and the Corner Office: What Lehman's 'Gorilla' CEO Has Lost*, ABC NEWS Business Unit, October 8, 2008, www.abcnews.com.
12. Richard Girgenti, commenting on *Integrity Survey 2008–2009*, KPMG LLP.
13. Ibid.

CHAPTER 2

The Politics of Banking Fraud

Chapter 1 briefly touched on the statistical and anecdotal evidence of America's gradual loss of its ethical virginity.

We turn now to the central and sensitive question of to what degree and how politics and its beloved offspring—bank regulation—contributed to the culture of fraud in the financial services industry, and in turn to its stunning demise in 2007–2008.

Politics and Regulation

Undoubtedly, one of the ground-breaking incidents of financial services fraud took place during the period of the Second United States Bank which, as discussed in the Introduction, was founded back in 1816 and promptly became brutalized by the shameless shenanigans of the heads of its Baltimore and Philadelphia branches.

In July 1836, President Andrew Jackson, leader of the Democratic Party, vetoed a bill to renew the Second Bank's charter and that put an end to the unbridled looting by its crooked executives. It also sidelined the prospects for implementation of central banking for 77 years.[1]

Not long after that, the "wildcat" banking frauds of the 1830s made the history books.

Today, bank regulation is shared by the states and the federal government. New York set up the very first banking authority under the Safety Fund Act of 1829. Three commissioners made on-the-spot investigations of every bank's affairs at least four times a year.[2]

Within a decade, New York's regulatory model was adopted by every New England state except New Hampshire.

Curiously, though, in 1843, the New York State Legislature abolished its commission, averring that its members were superfluous when bankers were honest and essentially ineffective when they weren't.[3]

The deregulation of New York banking however proved temporary. In 1851 the state set up a *permanent* banking department, followed shortly by Massachusetts. However, the newly created position of State Banking Superintendent came with the power to investigate a bank *only* if irregularity was suspected. Surprise audits—proven and powerful deterrents to would-be fraudsters in virtually all institutional environments—were strictly forbidden.

The political forces behind this dilution of state regulation are difficult to accurately assess, aside from the general fact that throughout the latter part of the nineteenth century, the political tug-of-war between state and federally-chartered (read regulated) banking was unceasing and frequently disruptive to financial markets.

Antebellum Banking

In the decade-plus period leading up to the Civil War, the forces favoring state-based "free banking" prevailed. The rise of free banking discussed in the Introduction shifted into high gear in the early 1850s, as did wildcat banking. The financial devastation visited on unassuming Americans was severe, yet it appears that in the early 1860s, the federal government showed no interest in (or perhaps lacked the ingenuity for) implementing stabilizing measures to protect consumers.

It took the start of the Civil War to force the government's hand, resulting in passage of the National Bank Act of 1863 which established the Comptroller of the Currency under the U.S. Treasury. Its mandate was to regulate the issuance of "greenbacks"—the new national currency—to help finance the federal government's war effort. The law required the national banks to purchase Treasury bonds which in turn provided the currency needed to finance the war effort.

However, with this came a new "hard core" devotion of Washington politicians to the concept of national banking and paper currency.

Thus, just after the War, Congress passed a law which imposed a ten percent tax on state banknotes. This effectively rendered most state banks uncompetitive with their national rivals. In 1860, according to the Federal Deposit Insurance Corporation (FDIC), there were 1,562 state banks. By 1865, the number had dwindled to 349.[4] Many of the well-capitalized state banks simply converted to national banks and began issuing national dollars instead of their own notes—which was the principal objective of the 1865 Act.

But the death knell for state banking was not to sound. Several years following the end of the Civil War, the politics of banking began to shift again. Despite Washington's commitment to the burgeoning national banking system, support for state banking remained vibrant. By 1871, state banks held nearly one-half of total commercial bank deposits.

As might have been expected, this persistent state-level opposition to the national banking system, in favor of a return to a decentralized, state-based system, spawned loud cries for repeal of the tax on state banknotes that was crippling so many of them.

The individual states, meanwhile took matters into their own hands by liberalizing the terms of state banking charters which fueled a significant spike in the number of new bank openings. In 1882, there were some 2,200 national banks and only 704 state banks. By 1885, the number of state banks had jumped to 1,015 and by 1900 the number had ballooned to 5,000, far outnumbering the 3,730 national banks in operation at the time.

Result: By the closing decade of the nineteenth century—a time of unprecedented industrial and population growth in the United States—the financial industry was defined by a thriving dual system of generally profitable national *and* state banks.[5]

Meanwhile, the foundation for modern financial and political influence over federal banking policy solidified over the early decades of the twentieth century—thanks in large measure to the tireless, if not somewhat self-serving push for central banking by a man named John Pierpont Morgan. Morgan had built the London-based business partnership of his father, Junius, with American banker extraordinaire George Peabody into the first major U.S. investment banking firm. The earlier mentioned depiction of Morgan by historian Charles Morris as a man of "absolute integrity" has not been uniformly shared.

Other historians have been rather less charitable to Morgan and his financial empire, chastising him for exploiting his estimable political power to strong-arm others into abandoning their opposition to his masterful formation of railroad and banking cartels.

Key to Morgan's grand scheme was creation of a federal centralized bank that would control monetary policy and, with a governing body stacked with cronies, would enable him and others like the Rockefellers to create market-dominating trusts in the rail, steel, banking, and other burgeoning industries. As economic historian Murray Rothbart wrote:

The financial elites of this country, notably the Morgan, Rock-efeller, and Kuhn, Loeb interests, were responsible for putting through the Federal Reserve System, as a governmentally created and sanctioned cartel device to enable the nation's banks to inflate the money supply in a coordinated fashion, without suffering quick retribution from depositors or note holders demanding cash.[6]

For better or worse, Morgan became one of the chief architects of modern securities markets. Under Morgan, *shareholders* actually became living, breathing investors to be reckoned with.

This admirable achievement was the product of Morgan's recapitalizing of the railroads with fresh money, much of it originating in Europe, where Morgan commanded enormous admiration and respect. He simplified the capital structure of the railroads into no more than two layers of debt with interest rates that the railroads' cash flows could comfortably manage. Equity meanwhile was sold to a broad market of eager investors.

And then came the Great War, with the Allies' massive need for credit. Almost overnight the dollar became the "modernized" world's currency of choice. For help in raising funds for their war efforts, France and Britain turned to JP Morgan. In what was at the time the largest bond issue ever, Morgan's financial empire orchestrated a $500 million debt offer, demonstrating politically correctness in deciding not to define the securities as "war bonds" to a public new to the securities game but instead as more palatable "trade finance" investments.

Early Due Diligence

The cultural and political origins of the financial industry's aversion to regulation can be found in the history of bank credit departments. The very idea of checking a prospective borrower's creditworthiness was anathema to bank executives throughout most of the nineteenth century. Hard as it may be for contemporary financial professionals to appreciate, until the early post-Civil War decades, business was done on the basis of trust. When a customer told a banker that he had 100 sacks of potatoes in a warehouse and wanted to borrow against them, the banker didn't dispatch an employee to confirm the existence or freshness of the collateral. It was simply assumed that the customer was telling the truth.

Problems arose however in the late 1800s when some of the expanding number of banks became too large for senior executives to know each of their customers personally. Together with the gradual increase in business complexity, this influenced a handful of banks to establish credit departments to review prospective borrowers' financial health prior to approval of loan applications. By 1910, most major banks had active credit departments and required loan applicants to supply financial statements became standard practice.

The nagging problem at the turn of the century was that American banking was no more stable than it was prior to the Civil War—which is not saying much. A great deal of the political wrangling over bank regulation was narrowly focused on the rules for establishing a bank, including how much capital would be required to open and operate one, whether it could issue paper currency or be required to demand loan repayments in gold or silver.

While there was a substantial increase in federal and state regulation between 1863 and 1910—most significantly, enactment of the National Bank Act, with its incentive for state banks to seek national charters—there was never a truly *consistent* regulatory framework for lending, capital requirements, or other key stabilizing factors.[7] It was no surprise, then that in the early years of the twentieth century, bank failures—a common fixture on the financial industry scene for decades—continued to accelerate.

Simultaneously, however, the growth of unregulated banking gave customers reason for concern about the stability of the institutions that were eagerly soliciting their deposits.

Result: The Office of the Comptroller of the Currency began to step up its examinations of national banks. While this gave the public a sense of enhanced confidence in the stability of the banking system, it soon turned out that their confidence was misplaced.

Reason: Most bank examinations proved to be shams. Examiner appointments were made on the basis of political influence and as such, most examinations were superficial at best.[8]

Business as usual remained uninterrupted and as one might expect, excessive risk and widespread fraud played major roles in day-to-day operations. In fact, the Comptroller of the Currency reported that fraud was among the leading causes of the rash of bank failures between 1865 and the early part of the twentieth century.[9]

This was fomented to a considerable degree by the ongoing monetary crisis involving silver, gold, and greenbacks in the years 1865–1873. In those years, it should be noted, government bond underwriting was essentially monopolized by two brothers, Henry and Jay Cooke. They played a central role in the creation of national banking in the early 1870s. Thereafter, they applied their underwriting talents to the financing of the Northern Pacific Railroad. This venture ultimately collapsed into bankruptcy under the weight of its proprietors' unbridled greed and the so-called House of Cooke investment firm quickly dissolved as well.

Some economic historians argue that this triggered what they term the Depression of 1873. Others suggest that such a crisis was little more than a myth. If nothing else, the Cooke calamity did contribute to the rapid reheating of the national debate over scrapping paper currency and returning to silver or gold. Indeed, each had short stints as the official currency of the country after 1873, only to be replaced by the political trade winds of the times which kept the country lurching from one standard to another well into the early part of the twentieth century.

Central Banking: The Drive Is Revived

As mentioned earlier, JP Morgan and his powerful financial and political cronies were instrumental in getting the Federal Reserve System established. However it is useful to note that the push for establishment of a *permanent and viable* central bank began in earnest in 1906 and underwent years of political wrangling. Influential investment banker, Jacob Schiff, the CEO of the prominent Wall Street firm Kuhn Loeb and Company, made a rousing case for a central banking institution at the New York Chamber of Commerce. This sparked a period of politicking during which members of the elite New York financial community would serve on a special Chamber commission to discuss and propose recommendations for currency reform to be overseen and controlled by a central bank. In the end, Schiff deferred to his friend, Isidore Straus, a Director of R.H. Macy, while the rest of the commission included two top executives of the JP Morgan empire, Frank Vanderlip, a top executive at the Rockefeller-controlled National City Bank of New York and Dumont Clarke, head of the American Exchange National Bank.

The august group soon issued a report which recommended the creation of a "central bank of issue under the control of the government." This was a direct attack on Treasury Secretary Leslie Shaw who was campaigning to have Treasury designated as the country's central bank.

The commission, however, along with the other reformers, denounced the Treasury for overinflating the economy by keeping interest rates dangerously low. Instead, the reformers argued

34

that a bona fide central bank would have much larger capital and undisputed control over the money market, and thus would be able to freely manage the discount rate to keep the economy under proper control. It was the commission's driving goal to establish "centralization of financial responsibility."[10]

Enter the ABA

The American Bankers Association (ABA) was founded in 1875 and in 1905 established its own "currency committee" which would also address the central bank debate. The problem for this 15-man commission was that there was no consensus on the formation of a central bank; yet the urgency of a national currency remained a central theme of the group's debate.

In late 1906, the ABA commission issued a report recommending broadening of national currency issued by the national banks, but *not* the creation of a central bank. The ongoing reluctance to make the leap to formation of a genuine federal bank was partly due to the earlier described rapid growth in the early 1900s of state banks. The national currency and banking reformers feared that this would undermine the efficacy of a central bank and therefore held off pressing its formation.

The debate was interrupted by a financial crisis in 1907, believed by some to have been brought on in large measure by the Treasury Department's inflationary policies of the years leading up to the crisis. This, it is suggested, helped to erode the public's confidence in the banking system with its absence of "a lender of last resort"—a frilly euphemism for "Federal Reserve."

The silver lining in all of this was that the Panic of 1907 forged a consensus on the central bank issue between banking and business leaders. What followed was an intense and lengthy campaign by Wall Street and business leaders to convince the general public of the prudence of establishing a central bank. This discussion was perpetuated in the halls of academia and by the press, with the *Wall Street Journal*'s editor, Thomas Wheelock cogently editorializing that "The market is volatile, because the small country banks are able to lend on that market, and their deposits in New York banks then rise and fall in uncontrolled fashion. Therefore, there must be central corporate control over country bank money in the call loan market."[11] Wheelock was no doubt referring to what Rothbart described as the "arbitrary credit-creation powers of the banking system"[12] which had prevailed throughout the 1890s and leading up to the 1907 crisis.

Political support for the central bank platform was enhanced when Comptroller of the Currency William Ridgely publicly endorsed the concept at just around the time the 1907 financial crisis was gaining momentum.

The Warburg Factor

Paul Warburg, who emigrated from Germany in 1902 after establishing himself as a successful banker in his family's firm of M.M. Warburg and Company, was among the most tenacious and vocal advocates of central banking in the United States almost from the day he stepped off the ship.

He quickly earned respectability through his friendship with Jacob Schiff, head of the influential Wall Street firm of Kuhn Loeb (Warburg had married Kuhn Loeb founder Solomon Loeb's daughter during an 1895 trip to New York).

Throughout the years, 1902 until the 1913 founding of the Federal Reserve, Warburg advocated tirelessly for the establishment of the central bank. Part of his zeal was derived from the notable, albeit short-lived success of the German Reichsbank which was credited with helping to maintain German monetary and economic stability in the late 1800s and early 1900s.

In March 1910, Warburg made a rousing speech that impressed the New York financial community no end. Entitled, "A United Reserve Bank for the United States," the address outlined among other things, the general structure of a proposed central bank. In addition, the banker argued that America's concept of a free and self-regulating market was obsolete, particularly in the money market. Instead, the action of the market must be replaced by what he termed "the best judgment of the best experts," in other words experts whose qualifications make them candidates to run a central United States bank.[13]

The following years were marked by multiple flips and flops in all corners of the American political system. The maneuvering over the structure, rules, and administrative details of the central bank, which engaged not only the political elite but also the financial heavy weights of Kuhn Loeb, JP Morgan, Rockefeller, and others finally resolved in the creation of the Federal Reserve Board and a network of regional Federal Reserve Banks.

The following 15 years, leading up to the Crash of 1929 were highlighted by a sustained and often rancorous rivalry between two American financial empires: One built around the "House of Morgan" and the other defined by an alliance between the Rockefeller oil dynasty, the W. Averell Harriman railroad cartel, and the mega-investment firm of Kuhn Loeb. This oligarchy of American finance was more influential than any other major industrial or financial institution in fueling the meteoric emergence of American industrialism. Through the completion of a modern continental railroad network, to the establishment of technologically advanced steel and automobile industries, not to mention the rapid expansion and increasingly sophisticated operations of the U.S. banking and investment banking business, these few elites created the foundations of what quickly became the world's unrivaled financial and economic superpower. With the exception of the interregnum of the Depression, this dominating stake in global economic and financial power was unshakeable and unbeatable. Until mid-2007, when the greatest crisis since the Depression brought the mighty American financial system to the precipice of total ruin.

Importantly, from the perspective of financial fraud and corruption, the 1929 Crash and subsequent Depression had their roots in regulatory systems not greatly unlike those in place when the 2008 crisis emerged.

Thanks in large measure to the unchallengeable power of the Morgan, Kuhn Loeb, Rockefeller, and other well-heeled financial bastions, together with the breed of industrial dynamos like Andrew Carnegie, John D. Rockefeller, Jay Gould, and James Hill, who came to be known as the "Robber Barons" and were targeted by Washington for potential break-up, financial markets remained generally unregulated throughout the 1920s. This, as discussed in the Introduction, is in large measure why egregious financial frauds in securities, lending, and general business practice came to tarnish the Roaring 1920s and helped to hasten the onset of the 1929 Crash.

It took the Pecora Commission, in the early 1930s, to sort out the tangled webs of fraud and deceit that had been perpetrated by top financial institutions and tolerated by so-called regulators.

As noted, the end result of the Pecora Commission's work was a swing of the regulatory and political pendulum back toward tight regulation, with passage of the Glass-Steagall Act, the Securities Acts of 1933 and 1934, and the accompanying establishment of the Securities and Exchange Commission (SEC).

A meltdown in the savings and loan industry (S&L), followed by a fresh wave of banking regulation, represents the last major banking and investment crisis before that which the United States wound up triggering in late 2008.

Financial Regulation Today

Today, despite the occasional noble efforts of Washington insiders such as John McCain, Russell Feingold and along with a few other well-meaning opponents of the seemingly indestructible infrastructure of special interest politics, elected officials, regulatory chieftains, and even White House movers and shakers have been notoriously susceptible to corruption by the powerful lobbying groups whose high-paid rainmakers roam the halls of political influence throughout the nation's capital.

The financial services industry, itself still among the most politically influential of any, is frequently criticized for what many view as a perpetuation of historically unfair and excessive sway in state and federal regulatory decision-making. With the House of Morgan's unbridled influence over American political and regulatory life in the 1920s having given the financial industry a reputation in some circles of being a juggernaut of corruption and greed, the image of Wall Street following the Crash of 2008 was eerily similar.

The most telling and nearly calamitous example of this historical similarity came as part of the subprime mortgage fiasco. For years following the S&L debacle, banking became gradually less regulated as banks found loopholes in the Glass-Steagall limitations on commingling of banking and securities activities.

As will be illustrated throughout this book, the greatest post-Depression act of deregulation of the financial services industry came in 1999 with the repeal of the Glass-Steagall Act, through enactment of the Gramm-Leach-Bliley Act. Formally known as the Banking Act of 1933, Glass-Steagall had erected a "wall" between investment banking and commercial banking, in an attempt to prevent a recurrence of the abusive conflicts of interest and frauds that characterized the laissez-faire financial services environment prevailing prior to the Great Depression.

According to a 1987 Congressional research report, the Glass-Steagall wall was designed to segregate the banking and securities businesses in order to "(1) maintain the integrity of the banking system; (2) prevent self-dealing and other financial abuses; and (3) limit stock market speculation."[14]

The report goes on to observe that:

In the nineteenth and early twentieth centuries, bankers and brokers were sometimes indistinguishable. Then, in the Great Depression after 1929, Congress examined the mixing of the 'commercial' and 'investment' banking industries that occurred in the 1920s. Hearings revealed conflicts of interest and fraud in some banking institutions' securities activities. A formidable barrier to the commingling of these activities under a single financial institution's roof was then established by Glass-Steagall. The Act consisted of four sections of the Banking Act of 1933. Most importantly, though, it contained language that made it a felony for anyone—banker, broker, dealer in securities, or savings institution—to engage in the deposit-taking and securities businesses at the same time.[15]

The banking industry's successful efforts to enlist the Clinton White House's influence in the debate over repeal of the Act thus represented the onset—perhaps inadvertent, perhaps not—of a period of financial deregulation that many analysts today metaphorically equate with the setting of a ticking time bomb that went off just when millions of new homeowners, institutional investors, and risk-prone financial institutions were standing on top of it.

In the prescient words of Paul Craig Roberts, Assistant Secretary of the Treasury under Ronald Reagan and a former *Wall Street Journal* editor:

"In 1933 the Glass-Steagall Act separated commercial banking from the securities business. It prevented securities speculation from destroying bank capital and shrinking

bank deposits from bank failures and runs on banks by depositors. Congress and President Bill Clinton foolishly repealed the Glass-Steagall Act in 1999. The repeal of the 1933 law was driven by profit lust in the banking industry and by "free market" ideology, which claims the unfettered marketplace is always superior to regulation. In pushing the repeal forward, Congress and Clinton ignored warnings from the General Accounting Office that the banks needed to build up their capital levels before being permitted to enter a broad range of securities businesses. The GAO also noted that there were no regulatory structures in place to monitor the new financial networks that would result from removing the wall between commercial and investment banking. However, greed and ideology won out over sound advice. The result is a crisis that, if mishandled, will be calamitous *[emphasis added]."*[16]

What If?

Could the subprime meltdown and the subsequent implosion of Wall Street, the U.S. banking industry, and essentially the better part of the entire U.S. economy have been averted with tighter regulation of lending practices, asset securitization, and hedge fund activity? Similarly, could what mortgage fraud expert, Michael S. Richardson calls the "American Epidemic" of mortgage fraud have been prevented with more restrictive rules governing real estate appraising, mortgage brokering, and loan underwriting?

Some would argue that had Clinton refused to repeal Glass-Steagall, he might have substantially inhibited the financial industry's headlong plunge into exotic derivatives, risky lending practices, and fraudulent mortgage brokering, appraising, and underwriting. However, the crisis involved far too many financial and economic forces to warrant such a simplistic explanation.

Nonetheless, had Glass-Steagall remained in place, the devastating impact of what in retrospect appears as a lethal absence of regulation would almost certainly have been significantly cushioned.

However, to avert the financial time bomb that did explode in 2007, such a regulatory void would at the very least have required a counteracting set of rules governing the securitization of mortgages—be they prime or subprime or anything in between.

For example, in the inimitably colorful phrasing of William Black, former General Counsel of the Federal Home Loan Bank of San Francisco, and Senior Deputy Chief Counsel, Office of Thrift Supervision and author of the widely acclaimed book, *The Best Way to Rob a Bank is to Own One*, the financial meltdown to a large extent stemmed from the widespread investment banking practice of putting together "... bad mortgages, [such as] liars' loans, and create[ing] the toxic waste of these derivatives.... And then they [the investment banks] sell it to the world and the world just thinks because it has a triple-A rating it must actually be safe. Well, instead, there are 60 and 80 percent losses on these things, because of course they, in reality, are toxic waste."[17]

Black was among the first financial industry gurus to ascribe a considerable share of the blame for the crisis to conflicts of interest in the securities rating system. In one of his especially direct analyses he said,

"The rating agencies never reviewed samples of loan files before giving AAA ratings to nonprime mortgage financial derivatives. The 'AAA' rating is supposed to indicate that there is virtually no credit risk—the risk is equivalent to U.S. government bonds, which finance refers to as 'risk-free.' We know that the rating agencies attained their lucrative profits because they gave AAA ratings to nonprime financial derivatives exposed to staggering default risk. A graph of their profits

in this era rises like a stairway to heaven. We also know that turning a blind eye to the mortgage fraud epidemic was the only way the rating agencies could hope to attain those profits. If they had reviewed even small samples of nonprime loans they would have had only two choices: (1) rating them as toxic waste, which would have made it impossible to sell the nonprime financial derivatives or (2) documenting that they were committing, and aiding and abetting, accounting control fraud."[18]

Numerous other respected securities lawyers, financial professionals, and former mortgage lenders have also expressed varying levels of concern or disapproval of the systematic failure of rating agencies to provide accurate (if unfavorable) analyses of the exotic derivatives backed by fraud-laden mortgages to the investing public. Notes the Financial Economists Roundtable (FER), a group of prestigious university economists:

"In the early 1930s, incentives for [Statistical Ratings Organizations (SROs)] to produce reliable information for investors were complicated by introducing ratings into the regulatory process. Regulators of banks, insurance companies, and pension funds began to use ratings to limit the riskiness of the assets held by regulated entities. Regulators now set two kinds of rules: rules that restrict the extent to which a firm can hold assets that fall below investment-grade or, as in the case of money market mutual funds, require a higher threshold than investment grade, and rules that link capital requirements to the ratings on individual securities, with lower capital charges for high-rated securities. The existence of such regulatory consequences was bound to intensify pressure on SROs to inflate the grades of lower-rated securities, because regulated clients routinely explore and develop ways of reducing their regulatory burdens. . . . As ratings became

more widely used in trigger clauses in bond contracts, strong ratings conveyed additional benefits to the issuer. . . . "

"The spread of photocopying technology facilitated unauthorized reproduction of SRO rating manuals, which undermined the traditional user-pays revenue model. SROs responded by shifting to a business plan in which the issuer pays for their services. This plan intensified SRO conflicts of interest with issuers. Issuers and underwriters actively shopped for ratings and were unwilling to pay for ratings they deemed too low. In the case of the newer securitized debt, pressure for favorable ratings has been particularly intense because the large underwriters of structured debt could direct substantial future revenue to a cooperative [Nationally Recognized SRO (NRSRO)], thus increasing the potential for undue influence."

"A further weakness inherent in issuer-pays arrangements is that they undercut SRO incentives to monitor and downgrade securities in the post-issuance market. The re-rating of securities is usually paid for by a maintenance fee that is collected in advance from each issuer."

"Few issuers are eager to be monitored closely, especially when monitoring is apt to result in downgrades, and so it is not surprising that ratings are seldom downgraded until long after public information has signaled an obvious deterioration in an issuer's probability of default."[19]

By the end of 2009, the SEC, the Obama White House, the Federal Reserve, and numerous legislators had proposed varying rules to re-regulate the ratings agencies. One thing which hardly anyone knowledgeable about the subprime meltdown disagrees with is that *some* sort of revision of the ratings system is not only inevitable but imperative.

Yet the current debate over regulatory reform does not end there. It is a virtual certainty that over the next few years, there will be vigorous debate over revising the rules governing bank underwriting of mortgage loans. And indeed, there should be. Though the collapses of Washington Mutual, Lehman Brothers, Bear Stearns, and numerous smaller financial institutions in late 2008 into 2009 triggered a retrenchment in mortgage lending standards to more responsible levels, history proves that the regulatory pendulum has momentum of its own and that the likelihood of another banking crisis is a virtual certainty sometime down the road, should politicians and regulators fail to put permanent preventive measures in place now. (Of course, as was evidenced by the repeal of the Glass-Steagall Act, any regulatory standards that are put into place now for the protection of investors could just as easily be repealed during the next financial boom and the political currents could flow again in favor of "less government").

Lynn Turner, former chief accountant of the SEC, aptly points out that the regulatory system that was in place in the years leading up to the financial crisis was not outdated; it was systematically dismantled by Washington. "They [Congress] passed the Gramm-Leach-Bliley Act, guaranteeing large financial supermarkets that can only be too big to fail, while prohibiting the SEC from being able to require regulation of investment bank holding companies. When legislation was passed saying one could put all these businesses under one roof, without a single word in the law requiring regulation of the inherent conflicts, it was sealed in stone that there would be huge institutions the government would have to bail out if they failed."[20]

Turner echoes Black in his observation that what resulted in the effective collapse of major financial institutions such as American International Group (AIG) and Enron was the introduction of credit derivatives that Congress and administrations ensured would never be subject to regulation. Turner further points out that AIG and others used such outlandish "products" as credit default swaps and so-called "structured" securities to avoid regulation, in the process writing a new chapter in U.S. financial history about how these products became what he terms financial "weapons of mass destruction." (More on this in Chapter 7.)

Thus, when AIG imploded in late 2008, suggests Turner, the federal government essentially had no choice other than to pour billions of taxpayer dollars into the failing insurance giant to stave off its total demise. In other words, the federal government created the financial environment that set the stage for massive abuse by massive financial institutions and is now on the hook to ensure that none of these self-made train wrecks is totally unsalvageable.

Is Regulation Here to Stay?

Banks require more regulation than most other industries because, as painfully demonstrated in 1929, an industry-wide run on banks can result in the collapse of the entire system literally overnight. Why is the prospect of a large-scale run on banks such a risk? Because the very people on whom the health of the system relies—depositors—typically have very little accurate information about the banks they do business with and as such, the failure of a major bank, or even mere rumors about financial problems at a bank can trigger a panic.[21] This is one key reason for the existence of federal deposit insurance (and helps to explain the federal government's quick action to boost this insurance from a maximum of $100,000 to $250,000 in late 2008 when it appeared that the U.S. financial system was on the brink of imploding). It is also the reason why the financial services industry is regulated by more agencies than any other.

The obvious next question is "If regulation is unavoidable, what type and how much is needed to keep the system stable and solvent without encumbering the financial institutions to the point of competitive disadvantage?" This is precisely the debate that the federal government became embroiled in once the proverbial dust began to settle after the $700 billion Troubled Asset Relief Program (TARP) bailout was put into place in late 2008. Proposals ranged from eliminating all of the existing banking regulatory agencies and replacing them with a single body to act as a "super-regulator" of all financial activity to a small group that advocates self-regulation.

Details of this debate and prospective solutions to the problem are discussed in Chapter 8.

Meanwhile, suffice it to say here that to the Obama Administration's credit, the historic bailout of the U.S. financial system through implementation of the outgoing Bush Administration's TARP did prevent the total collapse of any of the "too-big-to-fail" institutions such as Bank of America, JP Morgan Chase, AIG, and Citigroup. The disintegration of any of these institutions would undoubtedly have set off a global panic that may not have been controllable.

While, as later chapters will indicate, some financial market thought leaders argue that allowing one or more of these finance industry monoliths to fail would have been better for the financial system than investing hundreds of billions of taxpayer dollars into their *potential* survival, because of the current banking industry's intricate interconnectedness with financial institutions throughout the world, the real possibility of a worldwide run on banks was palpable. Such a catastrophe would have resulted in financial devastation far in excess of that envisioned by the kind of run described earlier in the context of depositors' lack of accurate information about the banking system.

Thus, while the political fallout from the TARP program set off a minor firestorm of outrage on the part of blue collar groups and die-hard free marketers, there is little doubt that without the prompt intervention of the federal government, the widely expressed fears of a modern-day Great Depression might have proved to be right on target.

Notes

1. John Steele, "A Short Banking History of the United States: Why Our System Is Prone to Panics," *The Wall Street Journal*, October 10, 2008.

2. Benjamin J. Klebaner, *American Commercial Banking: A History* (Boston, MA: Twayne Publishers, 1990), 44.

3. Ibid.

4. Federal Deposit Insurance Corporation, *FDIC: Learning Bank*, www.fdic.gov/about/learn/learning/when/1850-1899.html.

5. Benjamin J. Klebaner, *American Commercial Banking: A History* (Boston, MA: Twayne Publishers, 1990), 67–68.

6. Murray N. Rothbard, *A History of Money and Banking in the United States: Colonial Era to World War II* (Auburn, AL: Ludwig von Mises Institute, 2002), 258.

7. Kenneth Spong, *Banking Regulation Its Purposes, Implementation, and Effects*, report by the Division of Supervision and Risk Management Federal Reserve Bank of Kansas City 2000, 18–20.

8. Ibid., 100.

9. Shelagh Heffernan, Professor of Finance, Cass Business School, University of London, "The Causes of Bank Failures," A. W. Mullineux, Victor Murinde, Eds., *Handbook of International Banking*, (Williston, VT: Edward Elgar Publishing, 2003), 379.

10. Murray N. Rothbard, *A History of Money and Banking in The United States: The Colonial Era to World War II* (Auburn, AL: Ludwig von Mises Institute, 2002), 235–236.

11. Ibid., 242.

12. Ibid., 167

13. Ibid., 250.

14. William D. Jackson, *Glass-Steagall Act: Commercial vs. Investment Banking*, Economics Division Congressional Research Service, 1987, 3.

15. Ibid.

16. Paul Craig Roberts, *How to End the Subprime Crisis, Information Clearing House*, October 3, 2008, www.informationclearinghouse .info.

17. William K. Black, interviewed by Bill Moyers, *The Bill Moyers Journal*, April 2, 2009.

18. William K. Black, "The Two Documents Everyone Should Read to Better Understand the Crisis" *The Huffington Post*, March 28, 2009, www.huffingtonpost.com/william-k-black/the-two-documents-everyon_b_169813.html

19. "Statement on Reforming the Role of the Statistical Ratings Organizations in the Securitization Process," Financial Economists Roundtable, December 1, 2008, 3–5.

20. Lynn E. Turner, "The Systematic Dismantling of the System," *CPA Journal*, May 2009, 16–17.

21. Mullineux and Murinde, *Handbook*, 367–370.

CHAPTER 3

Modern Day Financial Services Fraud (1980–2010)

The broad historical framework of financial services fraud presented in the previous chapters is helpful in understanding the inevitability of various forms of illegal or unethical conduct in banking institutions. That fraud is intricately woven into the fabric of American financial history suggests that internal fraud fighters, regulators, and law enforcement agencies will be kept busy in perpetuity by the ensconced population of dishonest employees and managers at all levels and in all functions of financial services organizations.

It is, however, not unreasonable to hope for the evolution of a regulatory infrastructure that substantially mitigates some of the many fraud risks besetting banks today. The feasibility of such an effort was demonstrated in the wake of the Savings and Loan (S&L) crisis of the 1980s when at a cost of $150 billion to U.S. taxpayers, the federal government initiated its vast clean-up project that involved nearly 700 hundred failed S&Ls.

The legal vehicle for accomplishing this was the Financial Institutions Reform, Recovery, and Enforcement Act of 1989 (FIRREA). The law put thrifts under the regulatory umbrella of the Federal Deposit Insurance Corporation (FDIC) and other banking agencies. The minimum capital-to-asset ratio, which, at a mere 3 percent prior to the S&L debacle, and which ultimately enabled swashbuckling financial bosses to buy S&Ls with little or none of their own money, was bumped up to 8 percent. And of course the famed Resolution Trust Corporation (RTC) was set up with $50 billion in proceeds from government-sanctioned bond offerings and a mandate to take over insolvent banks, pay off the depositors, and sell off any assets that were worth anything.

Interestingly, the $150 billion cost of dispatching the S&L debacle—though three times the RTC's original estimate—seems trivial in the context of the $700 billion-plus bank bailout slammed through Congress in September 2008 when the collapse of Bear Stearns, Lehman Brothers, Washington Mutual, and other big-name financial institutions appeared to mark the beginning of the end for the American financial system.

Though it is unfortunate that throughout history, meaningful remedial measures have come into force only *after* damage has been done by financial fraudsters, the cliché, "better late than never" is especially fitting in this context.

The Fraud Culture and Today's Frauds

The "fraud culture" described in Chapter 1 must be more closely examined to fully understand the genesis of the major frauds that ravaged the U.S. economy beginning in the 1980s and then morphed into monstrous misdeeds and misjudgments that propelled the meltdown of 2007–2008.

After all, as will become clear, the latter did not evolve of its own independent forces. Without a doubt it did have its unique combination of destructive elements. But the early groundwork for the subprime meltdown, the high-risk strategies of Wall Street's elite, and the evaporation of trillions of dollars worth of American wealth in the short course of about 90 days was laid in the 1970s and 1980s when the future bosses of high finance were just graduating college.

The "Milken/Boesky" Era

Michael Milken for example may not have landed on Wall Street with the premeditated intention of perpetrating the biggest financial fraud in American history.

However the era of the late 1970s and early 1980s was one of regulatory nirvana for inventive Wall Street finance whizzes like Milken, Ivan Boesky, Martin Siegel, and a small clique of others.

What started as a modest Beverly Hills base for selling high-risk, high-yield bonds eventually grew into a veritable empire built on massive "junk bond" deals. While Milken's employer, Drexel Burnham Lambert, was initially reluctant to allow its young finance "revolutionary" to set up shop on the Pacific Coast, the hesitation soon dissipated as Milken gradually established himself as the firm's top rainmaker.

The only problem was that despite what some Milken contemporaries described as financial genius, the overpowering force of greed led Milken and his closest business associates down a path of brazenly illegal securities trading which ultimately earned Milken a 10-year sentence and a penalty payable to the government of $600 million (Milken actually only served two of the 10 years).

The trouble started well after Milken had established himself as a Wall Street renegade by raising hundreds of millions of dollars in high-yield debt—often to finance the hostile takeovers of large U.S. companies. While selling junk bonds is in and of itself perfectly legal, the problem arose when Milken, Boesky, and others engineered massive insider stock trades in connection with the takeover deals they were financing and manipulated the shares of companies that were targets of their high-stakes financing deals.

Among the numerous deals was the stock-manipulation scheme between Milken and Boesky in connection with the home-improvement company, Wickes which was emerging from bankruptcy and was seeking to raise capital for acquisitions. Through an intricate deal involving the issuance of common and preferred shares, Milken and Boesky, according to court documents, colluded in manipulating the price of Wickes stock to enable Wickes to divest itself of a sizeable chunk of preferred shares which required payment of dividends of 10 percent (equal to approximately $15 million in payments that Wickes chose to hold on to in order to engage in various takeover attempts).

At Milken's request, Boesky bought enough shares to push the price of Wickes shares high enough that, under the terms of its preferred share offer, all of the preferred shares would automatically convert to common shares, thereby releasing Wickes from its 10 percent dividend obligation. Meanwhile, Drexel was paid a tidy $118 million by Wickes for services rendered in connection with a number of acquisition attempts.[1]

Importantly, Milken's exploits in illegal stock trading were not terribly innovative to securities regulators at the Securities and Exchange Commission (SEC). Indeed, insider trading was added to the federal criminal code through the Securities Act of 1934. But Milken gave dramatic new meaning to the term and practice of illegal insider trading and the government finally caught up with him once it had nailed Boesky on massive illegal trading deals in collusion with Milken and got him to "flip" on his former cohort, known by then in the finance world as "the King."

The moral of the Milken-Boesky story which played out mainly in the 1980s is that it personified the "new greed" that swept Wall Street with the institutionalization of high-yield bond financing, leveraged buyouts, and ultimately brazenly illegal securities manipulation.

As Professors Stephen Rosoff, Henry Pontell, and Robert Tillman, co-authors of an important book on securities fraud wrote,

"... the 1980s have been viewed retrospectively as the decade when greed came out of the closet. The love of money, which once 'dared not speak its name,' refused to shut up. Nowhere was the new dignification of greed more pronounced or the spiraling decline of public trust more problematic than on Wall Street, which grew more and more estranged from Main Street."[2]

This unfortunate trend manifested itself in an explosion of Milken-like wheeling and dealing involving more and more Wall Street firms and of more and more 30-something baby boomers driven to become obscenely wealthy by mastering the art of what Rosoff, Pontell, and Tillman aptly termed "paper entrepreneurism."[3]

These were the years when BMWs became "must-have" status symbols for these modern-day financial fast-trackers. BMW had been exporting small numbers of sports sedans to the United States since the late 1960s. But only a miniscule contingent of mostly middle-aged quirky car freaks enamored with the storied history of the Bavarian Motor Works of Munich, Germany and who cherished the quality and outstanding engineering of these unique "performance" sedans purchased enough of the upstart company's rather pricey vehicles to earn it a speck on the map of the vast U.S. auto market. But by the late 1980s anyone who was anyone on Wall Street who *didn't* own a "Bimmer" was immediately dismissed as a loser.

The story encapsulates the emergence of the "me generation" of the 1980s, when fast money was the guiding light of financial industry baby boomers. Michael Milken and his clique of mega-fraudsters represented the extreme fringe of the new culture of unabashed avarice and frenzied pursuit of material status. But the mainstream contingent of youthful cash fiends did a fine job of laying the mental groundwork for what in the 1990s and early 2000s became the out-of-control age of derivatives which, as will soon become clear, were instrumental (no pun intended) in the ultimate implosion of the financial system. (The term "derivative" is defined by Professor Campbell R. Harvey, of Duke University as "A financial contract whose value is based on, or 'derived' from, a traditional security [such as a stock or bond], an asset, [such as a commodity], or a market index."[4])

Fancy Financing Foments More Fraud

It could reasonably be argued that Milken's junk bonds represented the primitive version of today's generation of ultra-complex derivatives such as mortgage-backed securities (MBSs), collateralized debt obligations (CDOs), collateralized mortgage obligations (CMOs) and the ultimate tools of potential utter financial destruction—credit default swaps (CDSs).

While the mechanics of junk bonds may be more readily understandable by investors than are today's derivatives, the opportunities for abuse have proved equally numerous and in many instances equally destructive for both types of securities.

The junk bonds of the 1980s soon got company from several new types of early derivatives, engineered primarily by Credit Suisse Financial Products (CSFP), the precursor to Credit Suisse First Boston. CSFP was led by another money-obsessed, yet somewhat less ostentatious figure than his 1980s predecessors named Allen Wheat. Wheat's tenure at CSFP saw the early 1990s invention and market blossoming of two new financing instruments: structured notes and structured finance.

Frank Partnoy, a former Wall Street securities trader and one of the true geniuses in the arcane nuances of derivatives, explains structured notes like this: "Unlike a typical bond, which has a series of standard coupon payments and then a fixed principal payment, a structured note's returns might vary wildly, based on different variables. In other words, the bond or note was structured so that its payouts were based *on any conceivable financial instrument or index* (emphasis added). One structured note was even linked to the number of victories by the Utah Jazz basketball team, although more typical variables were interest rates or currencies."[5]

By 1993 virtually every major bank was selling structured notes on behalf of *Fortune* 500 issuers such as General Electric, IBM, and DuPont. The spread of this popular financing vehicle was driven by their low cost compared to issuing conventional stocks or bonds.

Structured *finance*, meanwhile was the original product that gave rise to a variety of similar deals involving the now-common practice of repackaging existing securities to gain a higher rating from the rating agencies and then selling off *tranches*, or segments, of the securities at prices based on their actual level of riskiness.

For example in the late 1980s, derivatives financing took a major leap toward its current state of mind-numbing complexity with the invention of what came to be termed the collateralized bond obligation (CBO). The invention of CBOs is attributed by Partnoy to Fred Carr who was at the time head of an insurance company called First Executive Corp. Carr apparently drew some inspiration from the Milken method of risk marketing, and took it an important step further by bundling high-risk, high-yield bonds together with less risky paper into a "package" of collateral-backing securities whose totality was in effect larger than its parts in the sense that the less-risky bonds enabled the security product to earn a higher credit rating than the junk bonds would be given on their own. Because investors were allowed to buy "slices" of the bond, they were willing to pay more for the pieces of the bond separately than they would pay for the riskier junk bonds if sold intact.

The risky part of these and many related derivates of the late 1980s and early 1990s was engendered by the prospect that interest rates might not move in the direction required to generate increased value in the securities. For example, if you bought $1,000 worth of CBOs with coupons of 5 percent and interest rates headed downward, your investment would be worth more than $1,000 because buyers of the same securities at the lower interest rate were getting two percentage points (or 200 basis points) less in profit. Inversely, if, after you bought your 5 percent CBOs, interest rates jumped to 6 percent, your investment would suddenly be worth less.

This is essentially what happened with most early derivatives products. Bets were made by the leading Wall Street investment houses based on expectations of interest rate movements and, depending on actual fluctuations, the firms either earned huge profits or suffered devastating losses.

That is exactly what happened with Salomon Brothers when it lost $371 million in the first six months of 1994 in bond value following a half-point interest rate hike by the Federal Reserve (Fed) in May of that year.[6]

It is also what gave rise to one of the high-profile cases resulting from deceptive derivatives manipulation: That of New York's Bankers Trust (BT) which since the late-1980s and early 1990s had been masterminding complex corporate financings with derivatives as the primary instruments. One of BT's biggest deals involved the Ohio-based greeting card company, Gibson Greetings. In late 1991, Bankers Trust convinced Gibson Greetings to do two interest rate swaps for $30 million. Interest rate swaps were well-established financing tools by this time. In a typical deal (if there is such a thing on Wall Street), the BT arrangement was intended to help Gibson Greetings reduce the interest rate expenses on its debt by doing an interest rate swap with its long-time client. According to Partnoy, the deal was structured in such a way that Gibson could cut its interest expenses by agreeing to receive a fixed rate in its investment in exchange for paying a floating rate on its existing outstanding debt. The floating rate started off lower than the fixed rate because of the added risk Gibson was accepting to take on floating rate debt.[7]

This type of "plain vanilla" swap, as Partnoy refers to it, was nothing new at the time (1991). Gibson agreed to do two swaps with BT, each for $30 million. Essentially they were structured so that the difference between what Gibson received in interest in the first two of a five-year deal would be guaranteed to be higher than what it was paying on its debt. After that, Gibson would be paying a floating rate on its debt so that if interest rates declined, it would save proportionately more on its interest *payments*. However the second deal was much more complex than the first. In a nutshell, BT sold Gibson a deal that was based on the London Interbank Overnight Rate (LIBOR), but involved a mathematical structure that would cause Gibson to lose huge amounts of money if interest rates rose. Which of course is exactly what happened. Gibson lost nearly $1 million on its second swap deal with BT. This only spurred Gibson's financial executives to bet more—to recoup their losses. In the end, BT reportedly earned about $13 million on its Gibson swap deals. It isn't known exactly how much Gibson lost.

The key point is that BT was able to profit by out-mathemetizing its client. It could be argued that Gibson's financial executives should have known exactly what they were getting themselves into, but apparently, when the swaps started getting really bizarre—as in being structured based on arcane formulas involving LIBOR—it is arguable that only the most gifted of mathematical minds could comprehend the intricacies of the deals.

What did this mean in the "real world" of corporate finance? For one thing, according to Partnoy, the second Gibson deal was an exercise in pure greed on the part of the company's treasurer, James Johnsen, in that if rates declined, Johnsen would have essentially created a new profit center for Gibson. Unfortunately for him, his plan backfired.[8]

For the regulators, this and several other deals involving other *Fortune* 500 companies—including most prominently

Procter & Gamble (P&G), which sued BT, charging fraud in failing to disclose key information about two derivatives trades it sold to P&G—were a proverbial rude awakening. They had all been executed "under the radar" and when it was learned in Washington that big companies were losing big money on what amounted to a high-stakes gambling operation, equally big problems developed.

In connection with the Gibson swap deals, the SEC initiated an action against Gibson in which it stated:

> *During the period from October 1992 to March 1994, BT Securities' representatives misled Gibson about the value of the company's derivatives positions by providing Gibson with values that significantly understated the magnitude of Gibson's losses. As a result, Gibson remained unaware of the actual extent of its losses from derivatives transactions and continued to purchase derivatives from BT Securities. In addition, the valuations provided by BT Securities' representatives caused Gibson to make material understatements of the company's unrealized losses from derivatives transactions in its 1992 and 1993 notes to financial statements filed with the Commission.*[9]

The Commission settled with Gibson and Johnsen, along with CFO Ward Cavanagh by requiring Gibson to disclose changes in its derivatives positions in its SEC filings, as it had done for the three years leading up to the culmination of the fiasco. Ultimately the question of BT's fiduciary duty to its client, Gibson Greetings came to the forefront in a lawsuit by the latter against the former. It was settled out of court with BT paying a small fraction of what was potentially owed to Gibson in losses resulting from the swap deals.

However, the SEC was quickly joined by the Commodity Futures Trading Commission (CFTC) and the Federal Reserve

Bank of New York in taking regulatory actions that were meant to drastically curtail BT's derivatives activities.

Ironically, in the context of its risk management posture between 2001 and 2007, insurance giant American International Group (AIG)—vilified for its alleged excesses in the derivatives markets in that period to the point of forcing Washington to throw it a $180 billion life jacket—actually made prudent investment moves in the early 1990s, with the firm's founder and then-CEO, Maurice Greenberg, eschewing risky derivatives in 1993.[10]

That year can be marked as the beginning of the political debate over derivatives, which continues to this day. It was the year that Arthur Levitt began his seven-year-plus tenure as head of the SEC, a tenure during which the political currents would shift alternately with and against Wall Street's relentless drive for non-regulation of the derivatives business.

In 1993, regulation of U.S. securities markets was split between the SEC and the CFTC, each of which fought ferociously to outdo the other in currying the favor of Washington power brokers.

In another historical irony, President Obama's FDIC chief, Sheila Bair (originally appointed to that position in 2006 by President George W. Bush), was Clinton's chairperson of the CFTC in 1993 when she was quoted as saying "We have a strong affinity for derivatives at this agency. We like them."[11] The quote is uncharacteristic in light of the reputation that Bair acquired in subsequent years as a courageous champion of consumer and investor interests, vocally criticizing the excessive risks that major banks like Citicorp had taken in the years leading up to the financial crisis. By implication, Citicorp's aggressive investment strategy which put billions of dollars worth of ultra-risky debt-related securities on its books was a key element of the undue risk Bair referred to.

Back to 1993: Arthur Levitt was on the other side of the debate from Bair on the derivatives issue. He warned inexperienced investors to stay clear of them, mainly because, as he at one point told Congress, very little was known about the actual risk inherent in many of these new investment "products." The implication was that prospective investors ran too high a risk of being defrauded by the creators and marketers of these instruments and should "play it safe."

However, at that point, Levitt did little to prevent the onset of the snowball effect that began, coincidentally enough, with Wall Street's victory in two key political debates—one over the valuation of stock options and the other over the thorny accounting issue of valuing derivatives at prevailing fair market prices. In the latter instance, Wall Street persuaded lawmakers that being forced to mark derivatives contract values to market would create undue volatility in the market, even though allowing them to go "unmarked" left investors in the dark about the true value of these instruments.

The Ignominious Birth of "Pay for Performance"

In the case of stock options, Wall Street prevailed in its campaign to prevent options from being accounted for as expenses, arguing that being required to do so would limit their ability to implement true "pay for performance" compensation plans for executives.

And with that single political affirmation of the "pay for performance" approach to executive pay, the degradation of executive values was unleashed. It was, specifically, the decisive signal to Wall Street that the "anything goes" mindset discussed in Chapter 1 was free to flourish. With CEOs now ultra-motivated to increase short-term share prices in order to reap the potentially immense windfalls from exercising options purchased at discounted prices, behavior in the C-suite underwent a profound sea-change. As Partnoy aptly observes, the effect of stock option grants on the behavior of corporate executives "isn't pretty . . . the increase in the use of stock options coincided with a massive increase in accounting fraud by corporate executives, who benefitted from short-term increases in their stock prices."[12]

How massive the increase was is difficult to quantify. However, there is ample evidence from SEC archives indicating that granting of stock options was a frequent and routine executive compensation practice throughout much of the 1990s. That in and of itself was no problem. The problem—from a fraud perspective—developed when corporate compensation executives started illegally backdating the options grants so that the price at which executives were allowed to exercise their options was timed to coincide with previous share price lows, thus providing an immediate windfall due to the often substantially higher price at which the options were *actually* granted.

This is illegal in several ways: It is a violation of securities laws in that failure to report such backdating—which was almost always the case in the 1990s—is prohibited, as is failure by the corporation to record the value of the options as executive compensation expense. Moreover, most options backdating grants were in violation of tax laws because, as two experts in the field explain:

> *Three possible violations of the Internal Revenue Code ("Code") could create criminal liability for backdating: (1) exceeding the compensation deduction limits of Section 162(m), (2) failing to qualify options under the rules that govern incentive stock options in Section 422, and (3) violating the provisions of Section 409A regulating deferred compensation. Like securities fraud, the criminal tax fraud statutes require an intent element. . . . Therefore, to be criminally liable under the Code's criminal statutes, a person must*

"willfully attempt" . . . *to evade or defeat any tax imposed by [the federal government].*[13]

In a landmark options backdating case, the SEC filed a civil fraud complaint against three former senior executives of Comverse Technology, Inc., alleging that they engaged in a decade-long fraudulent scheme to grant undisclosed options to themselves and to others by backdating stock option grants to coincide with historically low closing prices of Comverse common stock.

The complaint alleged that from 1991 to 2002, Comverse's founder and former Chairman and CEO, Kobi Alexander, "repeatedly used hindsight" to select a date when the closing price of Comverse's common stock was at or near a quarterly or annual low. According to the SEC, Alexander then communicated this date and closing price to Comverse's former general counsel who, with the CEO's knowledge, created fraudulent company records indicating that a committee of Comverse's board of directors had actually approved the option grant on the date the CEO had picked.

According to the SEC, Alexander received some $6 million in illegal compensation as a result of the backdating scheme. Ultimately, Alexander was charged with 35 counts of mail fraud, wire fraud, securities fraud, money laundering, and then some. He promptly resigned from the $1.5 billion company he had built from scratch and fled to Namibia which has no extradition agreement with the United States.

Finally, when the Sarbanes-Oxley Act (SOX) was passed, it included a provision dramatically reforming the laws governing stock option grants. Specifically, starting in August 2002, companies that granted stock options to executives were required to file detailed reports of the grants with the SEC *within two days*. That effectively brought the fraudulent status quo of options abuse to a screeching halt. However, it has not completely eliminated the problem. According to well-respected research, an estimated 20 percent of corporations that grant stock options to their executives still violate SOX by failing to report their options grants. Whether the Congress will amend SOX to require same-day reporting remains to be seen, but some prominent analysts suggest that this is the only way to clamp down on ongoing violations of the law.

The problem of course is that, as wily compensation executives and lawyers have shown, where there's a will there's a way. As Partnoy observes, "Any appearance of control in today's financial markets is only an illusion."[14] The obviously highly desirable use of options backdating—be it a violation of legal and accounting standards or not—remains high on the wish list of public companies. That alone is distressing evidence that even with the implementation of strong legal prohibitions against fraudulent options granting and the attendant violations of financial reporting laws, the *spirit* of these laws remains anathema to C-level decision makers. This attitude dovetails with the corporate proclivity for numerous other forms of securities fraud and deception, as described above.

Risky . . . Riskier . . .

The legal stage was set for further corporate fraud when in 1994 Congress passed—and then overrode President Clinton's veto of—the Private Securities Litigation Reform Act of 1995 (PSLRA). Promoted by its authors, Thomas Bliley, Jack Fields, and Chris Cox as a way of limiting frivolous lawsuits, every Republican in the House of Representatives voted for it.

The key provisions include:

- A shortened statute of limitations for filing securities fraud lawsuits

- Restricted legal fees paid to lead plaintiffs
- Excised punitive damages provisions from securities law-suits

The end result was to make it more difficult for class action securities complaints to be sustained through the litigation process.

Which brings us to yet another irony in the recent history of high-profile fraud as it pressed the U.S. financial and economic systems closer and closer toward the brink. According to one of the most respected minds in the securities fraud field, Joseph Grundfest, a former SEC Commissioner and subsequently a professor at Stanford Law School, the PSLRA unintentionally resulted in the enhanced dominance of the community of plaintiffs' attorneys in the storied New York City firm of Milberg Weiss Bershad Hynes & Lerach. In testimony before the Subcommittee on Securities of the Committee on Banking, Housing, and Urban Affairs in July 1997, Grundfest stated that:

It was generally understood that prior to passage of the Reform Act a single law firm, Milberg Weiss Bershad Hynes & Lerach ("Milberg Weiss"), played a dominant role as plaintiffs' class action counsel. Milberg Weiss' appearance ratio nationwide stood at approximately 31 percent prior to the Reform Act.

Subsequent to passage of the Reform Act, Milberg Weiss appeared to become even more dominant in the class action securities process. Aggregating parallel federal and state activity, Milberg Weiss's appearance ratio in 1996 stood at about 59 percent nationwide and 83 percent in California. Milberg Weiss's increased significance can be explained by the fact that: (1) it was likely the best capitalized plaintiffs' firm and therefore best able to finance the delays associated with slower procedures under the Reform Act; (2) it had the most diversified portfolio of plaintiffs' claims and was therefore better able to absorb the risk associated with litigation under the new regime; and (3) it is best situated to initiate legal actions which helped to interpret the Reform Act's provisions in ways most beneficial to its own interests.[15]

Sadly, as has been voluminously documented, Milberg Weiss's senior partners went to jail and were forced to pay immense fines for criminal abuses of the legal system. Having held itself out as the champion of the "little guy"—the hapless individual investor who suffered at the hands of reckless or criminally culpable corporate giants—Milberg Weiss had, as Grundfest noted in 1997, become the top plaintiffs firm in the country.

Along the way, though, the firm's revered senior partners determined that in order to maintain its position at the top, it had to induce lawsuits that might otherwise never come to pass. To do so, the senior partners participated in a corruption scheme involving payments of millions of dollars to individuals in exchange for their agreement to act as lead plaintiffs in class action suits—a serious violation of criminal law.

A federal investigation led to the 2006 indictment of several Milberg Weiss partners, including founding partner, Melvyn Weiss, and the eventual guilty pleas of several others.

The event represented a decidedly insidious example of what was happening to the moral compass of American business and finance in the first decade of the twenty-first century. The contagion that had a few years earlier begun to emanate from the C-suites of Enron, WorldCom, Adelphia, Tyco, and others also infected law firms and Wall Street investment houses in ways never before seen or anticipated.

Thus, as Professor Grundfest pointed out, the PSLRA did indeed spur Milberg Weiss to, in his words, "internalize the externalities associated with the need to invest to create new precedent interpreting the Reform Act's novel provisions." The only problem is that the impressive innovativeness of the firm in maintaining its leading position in class action litigation was accompanied—or perhaps, more to the point, was fueled by—unbridled greed which in keeping with the pattern of ethical corruption evident in so many foregoing white-collar crime cases, emerged as a product of one or more of the Fraud Triangle components—pressure, opportunity, and rationalization.

Meanwhile, it appears the PSLRA may be largely to blame for the significant increase in corporate financial frauds starting in 1995 and leading steadily to the history-making mega-cases of the Enron variety in 2002.

Specifically, as some experts argue, the Act emboldened C-suite occupants to bend the accounting rules, persuaded that they could now do so with impunity, as the new restrictions on shareholder lawsuits would shield them from challenges to their questionable bean-counting activities.

This apparent "warm-up" to the mega-scandals of the early 2000s was defined by some quite amazing frauds that in retrospect make Enron, Tyco, Global Crossing, and WorldCom appear less incredulous than they came to be.

For example, take the infamous fraudulent reporting scandal involving Stamford, Connecticut-based CUC. For more than 10 years CUC, at its CEO, Walter Forbes's instigation, inflated its earnings and understated its liabilities to convince analysts to continue recommending the company's stock as a "buy."

At the time (the late 1980's and early 1990's), the CUC case was the largest financial accounting fraud in history. Though the intricacies of the fraud are numerous and largely uninteresting, it is not difficult to guess exactly why Forbes, who had built the largest consumer products club in America would go to the lengths he did to so brazenly and persistently cook the company's books.

Of course, as mentioned above, the illusion of immunity from legal action established by the PSLRA likely played an indirect, if not subconscious role in motivating Forbes to perpetrate the fraud. And, as many analysts of the CUC case have noted, Forbes's greed-driven desire to protect the value of his hard-won millions worth of CUC stock played no small part in the convoluted actions that ultimately led to his 2008 sentencing to 151 months in jail and order to pay restitution of $3.2 billion.

Essentially, the CUC fraud started out modestly. By the time regulators and law enforcement agencies got locked into investigating the case, the company was no longer called CUC. As summarized in a June 2000 SEC document describing its charges against the company's top executives: "Cendant was created through the December 1997 merger of CUC and HFS Incorporated. These proceedings and litigation are the result of the Commission's continuing investigation of a long-running financial fraud that began at CUC in the 1980s and continued until its discovery and disclosure by Cendant in April, 1998."[16]

Essentially, the merger was engineered by Forbes as a way of perpetrating a financial fraud that he had initiated years earlier by prematurely recognizing sales revenue and postponing recognition of expenses. This garden variety grew rapidly in the late 1980s and early 1990s when CUC's customer base—made up of members of consumer clubs much like Book-of-the-Month and related clubs.

But by the mid 1990s, growth had slowed, though thanks to years of book-cooking, it appeared to Wall Street that CUC's earnings were on a steady upward trend.

By 1995, all of the expenses that should have been recognized by the company earlier were coming due. Forbes found himself in a cash bind so he forged a merger with hotel franchise owner, HFC Corp. The merger resulted in renaming the company Cendant and enabled Forbes to classify massive amounts of "expenses" as merger expenses, thereby enabling him to continue pushing out to the future the company's *actual* mounting losses.

Once the SEC started sinking its teeth into Cendant's books and those of its predecessors, it learned that virtually all of the company's C-level officers were in one way or another involved in the fraud. It was not until over a year later that CEO Forbes was finally indicted on civil fraud charges. But in the year or so leading up to that, Forbes watched most of his top lieutenants get nailed by the SEC. For example, in the February 2000 indictment:

- Cendant CFO, Cosmo Corigliano was charged with creating and maintaining a schedule that management used to track the progress of their fraud. Corigliano regularly directed CUC financial reporting managers to make unsupported alterations to the company's quarterly and annual financial results. The SEC stated that Corigliano profited from his illegal actions by selling CUC and Cendant at inflated prices "while the fraud he helped engineer was underway and undisclosed."[17]
- Anne Pember, the former CUC Controller, was the CUC officer described by the SEC as having been most responsible for implementing directives from Corigliano aimed at perpetuating the fraud. Specifically, the SEC charged Pember with implementing directives that inflated Cendant's annual income by more than $100 million, primarily through improper use of the company's reserves.
- Casper Sabatino, a former CUC vice president of Accounting and Financial Reporting, implemented directives from Corigliano to instruct lower-level CUC financial reporting managers to make Corigliano's requested alterations to the company's quarterly financial results.

Cendant's share price plunged from around $37 just before the company's 1998 admission of accounting irregularities to around $11 shortly thereafter.

This stunning evaporation of market capitalization due to a financial fraud was unprecedented and Wall Street didn't quite know what to make of it. In retrospect, however, the Street proved undaunted by the Cendant crisis, as the emergence of numerous comparably out-sized financial frauds would demonstrate.

At the time that the SEC announced its initial charges in the CUC-Cendant case, then Commission Enforcement Director, Richard H. Walker said, "Today's [SEC enforcement] actions make crystal clear that the SEC and the U.S. Attorney have zero tolerance for fraudulent financial reporting. Financial fraud causes grave harm to the investing public and undermines the integrity of our capital markets. Investors need to know that when they invest their hard-earned dollars in a company's stock, they can depend on the reliability and accuracy of the financial information that the company reports about its operations."[18]

Ten years hence, Walker's words ring disturbingly hollow. Though they were uttered just two years prior to enactment of the Sarbanes-Oxley Act, the prevalence of financial reporting crimes as the second decade of the twenty-first century commences causes one to wonder whether the day will ever come when the incumbent SEC Enforcement Director will be able to announce that the Commission's work, in cooperation with federal law enforcement and other regulators have finally succeeded in putting teeth into the legal and regulatory arsenal against financial fraud. And that the frequency of such crimes and the dollar losses attributable to them have begun to decline.

It would be a full 10 years, and three trials subsequent to the SEC's initial public statements about its enforcement actions that Forbes would finally be sentenced for his crimes. But the key lesson is that the CUC-Cendant fraud represented a landmark case in that it was the first in modern financial history to involve such a long-standing, egregious, and costly combination of financial crimes. It would not be long before other *Fortune* 500 CEOs followed in Forbes's footsteps, clearly demonstrating that the prospect of a stiff sentence for such activities was no deterrent to engaging in them.

It can thus be argued that the erosion of senior executive ethics that gained momentum in the 1990s and early 2000s played at least an indirect role in bringing on the eventual financial crisis of 2007–2008. After all, had there been no Cendant, no Enron, no WorldCom, and so on, perhaps Wall Street would not have been as prone to push the limits of ethical financing conduct with its creation and aggressive marketing of investment "products" that, as will soon be discussed, became the dangerous weapons that blew up the financial system.

For example, at the time that the Cendant case was going on the great rise of the CBO market well underway and these derivatives were being traded as a matter of routine daily Wall Street business.

As you might expect, after CBOs became all the rage among the big Wall Street firms, some of the bonds naturally went south as a result of major defaults on some of the underlying junk bonds. It was, however, far from automatic that the three major rating agencies adjusted their ratings on the securities downward. Moody's, S&P, and Fitch had in fact helped the CBO market mature by buying into the concept of CBOs: namely, that by bundling low-rated (junk) bonds together with better-rated ones, the total became an attractively-rated bond, despite the existence of the low-grade stuff. That enabled bond traders to sell securities for more than buyers would otherwise be willing to pay for the bonds separately. But when some of the big CBO deals fell apart due to defaults, the credit rating agencies were reluctant to downgrade the securities, knowing that the owners would end up with enormous losses.

However, while some regulators warned of impending disaster with CBOs and other junk bonds, most of these deals remained beyond the reach of the Fed, the SEC, and other regulatory bodies.

By 1994, meanwhile, CMOs, swaps, structured notes, and other derivatives were experiencing a similar surge in popularity. CMOs were not considered junk bonds because they were backed by the U.S. government. That's because the most basic variety of CMOs were backed up low-risk, "prime" mortgages. But it took little time for Wall Street to begin finagling these securities, creating them with mortgages of less creditworthy borrowers and thus introducing considerable volatility to the overall CMO market.

Meanwhile, the previously described derivatives—structured notes, swaps, and so on—were being bought by the billions by mainstream institutional investors, most notably the Treasurer of Orange County, California, Robert Citron. Citron, apparently bent on outperforming his peers at other municipal finance shops, was among the first to plunk down taxpayer cash on securities that were substantially riskier than the traditional U.S. Treasury and money market vehicles in which most responsible public treasurers parked their taxpayers' money.

In the early 1990s, Citron accumulated as much as $20 billion in structured notes. At the time interest rates were low. The Federal funds rate had declined steadily from a peak of $9\,^3/_4$ in late 1987 to 3 percent on September 4, 1991. The Fed didn't change that rate throughout 1992 or 1993. After such a long run of declining rates and no apparent reason for the Fed to change its course, traders and investment strategists at all of the major Wall Street firms were brimming with confidence about making investments in derivatives based on the virtual certainty that rates would remain low. The dollar signs were flashing brightly among traders up and down Wall Street, as they bought up more and more structured notes and convinced some of their biggest institutional clients to do the same. The only catch was that, like the trap that James Johnsen fell into at Gibson Greetings, the securities being sold to investors were structured in such a way that if interest rates went lower, the investors would earn profits, but if they went up, the losses would be exponentially higher. The investment firms that sold the securities didn't care; they had already pocketed their tens of millions in fees.

Thus, as anyone uninfected by the greed bug would have predicted, the day of reckoning finally arrived. When on February 4, 1994 Fed Chairman Alan Greenspan raised rates from 3 percent to $3\frac{1}{4}$ percent—the first increase since January 1988—it came as a shock to everyone who had been betting big on continued low rates. That quarter-point hike in rates wiped out billions of dollars of profit for Wall Street firms as well as for Orange County, California and numerous other smaller municipalities whose treasurers had also been convinced by smooth-talking Wall Street marketers to drink the derivatives Kool-Aid beginning in the early 1990s.

But the Orange County situation was more complex—and much more ethically reprehensible. Though Merrill Lynch, Orange County's prime investment bankers, along with the other big Wall Street firms, knew well that they were pulling a fast one over on their clients by misrepresenting—or at least under-representing—the underlying risk in the structured instruments they were selling, they continued to peddle them to anyone who would buy them. Adding more TNT to the time bomb were the rating agencies which were paid handsomely to bless the deceptive "products" being hawked with AAA ratings—the same rating, says Partnoy, given to securities of much lower risk.[19]

Coincidentally, shortly after the Clinton Administration set the foundation for securities havoc by repealing the Glass-Steagall Act in 1999 (see Chapter 6), Wall Street was pressing for even *more* freedom to sell products that nobody understood but that would potentially earn the big trading houses astronomical profits.

In 2000, the Commodity Futures Modernization Act (CFMA) was passed. According to a segment on CBS News's *60 Minutes*, "[this law] not only removed derivatives and credit default swaps from the purview of federal oversight, on page 262 of the legislation, Congress preempted the states from enforcing existing gambling and bucket shop laws against Wall Street."[20]

This was the equivalent of legalizing a form of gambling that had been rendered illegal in the early 1900s. New, ultra-sophisticated (or complex depending on your point of view) securities could now be legally traded over-the-counter (OTC).

The *60 Minutes* segment was referring to the set of laws on the books that had banned the primitive predecessors to modern derivatives markets called bucket shops. Bucket shops cropped up throughout the United States in the 1880s and took a form not unlike what are commonly known today as boiler rooms. The bucket shop operators sold side bets to customers—usually gamblers and other risk-oriented individuals who wagered on shifts in stock prices on legitimate exchanges. But there were no actual securities involved and the unregulated nature of the market gave rise to an informal industry made of up scam artists and market manipulators eager to separate "customers" from their cash.

Bucket shops were shut down in New York by a 1908 law, in large measure due to their perceived contribution to the Wall Street panic of 1907. By 1920 most states banned bucket shops completely.

In the *60 Minutes* piece, New York Insurance Superintendent, Eric Dinallo retraced history by saying "[Bucket shops were b]etting parlors. It was a felony. Well, it was a felony when a law came into effect because it had brought down the market in 1907. And they said, 'we're not gonna let this happen again.' And then 100 years later in 2000, we rolled [the legal prohibitions] all back."

In retrospect, according to *60 Minutes*, "giving Wall Street immunity from state gambling laws and legalizing activity that had been banned for most of the 20th century should have given lawmakers pause. But on the last day and the last vote of the lame duck 106th Congress, Wall Street got what it wanted when the Senate passed the bill unanimously."[21]

A Deluge of Derivatives

Thus, the Clinton Administration left Washington having bestowed upon Wall Street's high rollers a license to run the derivatives markets anyway they pleased. The result was an explosion of new forms of derivatives and the meteoric expansion of markets for trading in the most complex and exotic of these products, none more potentially risky than credit default swaps (CDSs).

CDSs are actually not that complex, even though like the side bets placed with the shady operators of the bygone bucket shops, CDSs were not actual securities. At first, they were simple insurance contracts that promised the buyer a payout of a specified amount if the debt instruments upon which the contracts were based went into default. In this sense, they were extremely useful products for hedging the risk of default by a specific borrower.

According to one account, the first "real" CDS was developed in 1993–1994 by JP Morgan & Co. whose long-time client, Exxon Corporation had just experienced the worst tanker spill in U.S. history when the *Exxon Valdez* ran aground in Alaska. Exxon was slapped with a $5 billion fine and the company asked its trusty banker, JP Morgan for a line of credit of $4.8 billion to help pay it. The culture on Wall Street at the time was that you don't turn your back on a valued customer, so JP Morgan felt it couldn't say no to the request, even though the $4.8 billion loan would push the bank up against regulatory minimal capital reserve requirements. So the bank started looking for a way to keep the Exxon loan on its books but without the risk that Exxon might default. It offered to pay the European Bank for Reconstruction and Development (EBRD) attractive fees if it would commit to making good on the Exxon loan should Exxon default—an eventuality that both institutions considered highly remote. With the assistance of a small army of attorneys, the deal went through and the first credit default swap became a part of international financial history.[22]

From there, the credit derivatives market evolved with blistering speed, incorporating a plethora of variations on the original CDS theme. However, to this day, JP Morgan is considered the inventor of the CDS. And for 10 years, there was no reason not to bestow praise on the firm for its contribution to the American financial system's advancement into new realms of credit market efficiency and profitability. Little did anyone know back in 1995 that by 2007, some $62 *trillion* in credit default swaps would have been issued, up an astounding $50 trillion from just two years earlier.

Little, for that matter, did anyone know in 1995 that the explosion in CDS markets would culminate with the near-collapse of its biggest and boldest participant—AIG—as well as that of the entire global financial system. More on this in Chapter 7.

The Good Side of CDSs

Credit default swaps were critical to the financing (though *not* the collapses) of Enron, WorldCom, and other huge companies. Banks such as JPMorgan Chase and Citigroup that loaned billions of dollars to such companies found that they could greatly reduce the risks of these borrowers defaulting by using CDSs.

For example, as Frank Partnoy explains, "From August 2000 to May 2001, Citigroup created a series of Special Purpose Entities (SPEs), (special off-balance-sheet legal entities) [similar to the SPV's mentioned in the Introduction] that held AAA-rated bonds and issued a special type of credit derivative that depended on whether Enron defaulted. If Enron paid its debts, the investors [in the SPE] would keep the AAA-rated bonds. But if Enron did not pay, Citigroup would take the AAA-rated bonds and replace them with Enron's bonds. By using these transactions, Citigroup hedged its entire $1.2 billion [loan] exposure to Enron. Citigroup lost nothing when Enron defaulted in December 2001. Instead, the investors in Citigroup's SPEs were left holding the bag."[23]

While this was a wondrous piece of financial engineering on Citigroup's part, the question of the riskiness of CDSs had already arisen. Because the CDS market was relatively new in the late 1990s, senior financial officials began to voice concern that institutions that began buying or "taking positions in" CDSs might not fully understand the nature of the risks they were buying into. It was one thing for Citigroup to hedge its loan exposure to a direct client using CDSs, but it was quite another for a third party, such as a large insurance company or other financial institution, to purchase CDSs that were written against the debt of unrelated borrowers with minimal knowledge of that entity's financial condition, let alone the risk level of the debt against whose default the investing institution was betting.

Nonetheless, the market for CDSs grew rapidly in the late 1990s and early 2000s, with insurance companies, banks, investment banks, and even pension funds loading up on these potentially dangerous instruments. Making matters even more risky was the fact that one of the key motives for insurance companies and other institutions to invest in CDSs was that these securities were totally unregulated and doing so enabled them to engage in investment "opportunities" that insurance regulations generally prohibited.

Key among the "other securities" referred to above were instruments that in reality weren't *real* securities. They were called "synthetic collateralized debt obligations" and were sold based on the expectation that the *real* collateral—such as loans or bonds—would not go into default. *Actual* collateralized debt obligations—CDOs—were backed by *actual* loans that, like CDSs, were sold to SPEs. They were then divided into slices, each with a different level of default risk. According to one estimate, by 2002 there were $500 billion of CDOs.[24]

But the next level of financial precariousness belonged to synthetic CDOs. They were backed not by loans or bonds like conventional CDOs, but by CDSs. That made for a situation in which companies whose debt was the basis for the CDSs had no idea that investors were buying and selling CDOs based on those swaps—and vice versa. It was these synthetic CDOs that raised the most concern about excessive financial market risk on the part of seasoned Wall Street risk specialists and numerous other qualified observers.

As discussed in detail in Chapter 7, "regular" CDOs were somewhat more tangible as securities than their synthetic cousins, but they became highly risky in that many of the loans used as collateral eventually were subprime loans taken on by homeowners with sketchy credit histories.

Sound familiar? The fiasco in derivatives of the early 1990s is powerful proof that the syndrome of boom and bust in new derivatives by no means started with the 2006 meltdown of the subprime mortgage derivatives market which was so tragically fueled by the same type of complex securities but with far more widespread ignorance among their buyers about the real level of risk underlying them. Small wonder that the derivatives house of cards built with the flimsy glue of ever-expanding volumes of largely fraudulent subprime mortgages and brazenly deceptive securities sales tactics brought down with it the likes of Bear Stearns, Lehman Brothers, and Merrill—all of which held immense volumes of these securities.

Shortening Memories

Especially amazing is how effective greed is at shortening memories. After the 1994 derivatives debacle, no one went to jail. Robert Citron, after taking the blame for Orange County's ignominious bankruptcy in December 1994 was charged with several felonies, but ultimately paid a $100,000 and spent less than a year under house arrest.[25]

The only meaningful punitive repercussion from the disaster was the 1998 $400 million settlement by Merrill Lynch of a lawsuit by Orange County, claiming deception in the sale of the derivatives that Citron so voraciously purchased.

But how long did it take Merrill and its Wall Street rivals to get back, full throttle, into the derivatives game? Not long at all. The next wave of legalized betting with other peoples' money—replete with its seemingly built-in element of sleaze and deception—was already in its formative stages. In fact this time, the United States would be hit by a double-whammy. First came the wave of history-making corporate financial frauds, highlighted by Enron, but preceded by some equally horrific crimes. The second of course was the Great Meltdown of 2007–2009, the origins of which were established in the mid-1990s when the greatest run-up in residential housing prices got started in earnest.

The latter calamity will be analyzed in detail in Chapter 7. However, in the context of modern financial crime, it should be noted that the sea of fraudulent mortgages and ethically-questionable marketing tactics of high-risk derivatives issuers of the 2000s might not have been as calamitous as it was, had it not been for the fraying of American business ethics that, as should by now be clear, gathered momentum beginning with the Milken period and accelerated without interruption through the Cendant and Enron eras.

In this context, it is helpful to note that the SEC's docket of financial reporting fraud cases didn't start becoming noticeably lengthy until the late-1990s. Similarly, the Association of Certified Fraud Examiners (ACFE) has reported that in 2001 the percentage of total financial statement fraud cases studied totaled approximately 5 percent of the total number of cases examined (33 out of 660). In 2002, the percentage had risen to 8 percent, (40 cases out of a total of 508). By 2006, the Association reviewed 110 cases of financial statement fraud (11 percent of the total), while in the following year, the percentage remained generally unchanged, as fewer total cases were reviewed, of which 99 were financial statement frauds.

This trend is based on the ACFE's research of 21 different industries. The industry with the largest percentage of cases of financial statement fraud in recent years has been telecommunications, with 25 percent of total fraud cases. Financial services falls a bit further down the list at 12.9 percent, but is substantially harder hit by these crimes than, for example, real estate and construction, at 3.4 percent and 7.1 percent respectively.

Importantly, the ACFE in its most recent research, reports that internal controls over financial reporting (ICFR), as prescribed by Sarbanes-Oxley, have *not* resulted in a reduction in losses to financial statement fraud. On the contrary, the ACFE states in its *2008 Report to the Nation on Occupational Fraud:*

> *We found that the presence of these controls was not correlated to a decrease in the median loss for financial statement fraud schemes; in fact, for all controls except hotlines, the converse was true. Organizations with these controls in*

place experienced greater fraudulent financial statement manipulations than organizations lacking these controls. Additionally, organizations that had independent audit committees and those whose management certified the financial statements actually took longer to detect the fraudulent financial misstatements than their counterparts without such controls.[26]

These conclusions are clearly evident in Exhibit 3.1.

The ACFE's data on financial statement fraud comprise five main categories of such fraud:

1. Concealed liabilities
2. Fictitious revenue
3. Asset valuations
4. Improper disclosure
5. Timing differences

The data clearly indicate that not only did SOX fail to deter corporate book-cooking, it appears to have been no obstacle at all to determined executives. Though difficult to prove, it is probably safe to suggest that the reason for the continued rise in financial statement fraud lies in the earlier-discussed factors of intensifying competitive pressure on executives to meet the numbers, together with greed and lack of commitment to the organization's long-term financial health.

With regard to the financial services industry specifically, the data on financial statement fraud suggest that this particular variety of internal crime continues to pose a dire threat to the financial industry's stability, financial health, and reputational integrity. With the trauma of the financial industry meltdown to go on, it is certain that the regulatory pendulum will swing decisively back toward tighter oversight of banking which, it can only be hoped, will provide the deterrent to rising financial

EXHIBIT 3.1 Sox-Related Internal Controls in Financial Statement Fraud Cases

Sox-Related Internal Controls in Financial Statement Fraud Cases (99 cases)										
Control	Control in Place?				Median Loss			Months to Detection		
	Yes		No		Yes	No	% Reduction	Yes	No	% Reduction
Management Certification of F/S	53	53.5%	32	32.3%	$3,500,000	$1,300,000	−169.2%	33	28	−17.9%
External Audit of ICOFR	41	41.4%	40	40.4%	$3,250,000	$1,868,000	−74.0%	24	30	20.0%
Independent Audit Committee	40	40.4%	47	47.5%	$7,000,000	$1,500,000	−366.7%	36	30	−20.0%
Management Review of IC	34	34.3%	43	43.4%	$3,000,000	$2,000,000	−50.0%	25	30	16.7%
Hotline	24	24.2%	53	53.5%	$2,000,000	$2,500,000	20.0%	26	30	13.3%

statement fraud in the industry that SOX was evidently unable to furnish.

Enron et al.

Contrary to popular belief, the Enron bankruptcy was of the typical corporate variety, sort of like General Motors, Chrysler, or in earlier years, the oil giant, Texaco in 1987, or any of hundreds of Silicon Valley "dot-com" disasters throughout the 1990s.

In fact, Enron's collapse was due in large measure to unregulated securities trading, with off-balance sheet Special Purpose Entities (SPEs) created by CFO Andrew Fastow in which he personally had financial interests and, oddly, about which the late CEO, Kenneth Lay actually knew comparatively little. By the time Enron imploded, Lay had extracted himself from much of the day-to-day operations of Enron, preferring instead to hobknob with Texas political big-wigs like the George H. W. Bush family, senators, congressmen, and the like.

Meanwhile back at the proverbial ranch, COO Jeff Skilling and Andy Fastow were hard at work in the late 1990s cooking up fantastically innovative financial deals that had little if anything to do with oil—the company's original business. Instead, they pursued electricity deals that exploited the energy crisis in California, as well as telecommunications transactions and, perhaps most bizarrely, trading in weather-related derivatives. These were bets on minimum or maximum temperature in specific locations, or the amount of expected rain or snowfall.[27]

Financing for most of these endeavors was arranged by Fastow through a variety of derivatives-based transactions, mostly off-balance sheet and therefore hidden from shareholders and regulators.

But when the public and the rating agencies learned about some of the sleazier deals that Enron had been running, especially the multi-million-dollar rip-off of California via a trading scheme that resulted in the manipulation of the West Coast energy market and, some argued, outright price gouging of California residents, they downgraded Enron's credit rating which essentially locked the company out of the credit markets, thus dooming its entire trading operation. Within a week Enron had filed for bankruptcy protection.

While Citigroup and JPMorgan Chase continued to extend credit to Enron even after it had filed for bankruptcy, presumably hoping that doing so would buy time for Enron to repay its loans, the legality of the banks' financial relationship with Enron was never questioned by investigators or prosecutors. Even financial industry regulators didn't raise much of a fuss about various off-balance-sheet deals that Enron was perpetuating.

Nor for that matter did many of the derivatives deals that Enron had initiated come under scrutiny, given that technically, they were not illegal, though they certainly raised serious questions about compliance with the *spirit* of the law and the ethical propriety of many of these arrangements, given their brazen deceptiveness.

Unfortunately, the Enron financial fraud case was not an isolated incident in the 2000–2002 period. It was soon followed by comparably massive fraud-driven bankruptcies at Adelphia, Global Crossing, and, most notably WorldCom. In these and other collapses, the financial frauds that fueled them were generally not as convoluted or arcane as those concocted by Enron's Fastow. Yet, the end result of the rash of dirty financing cases changed the mindset of the entire financial services industry forever.

For example, as alluded to in Chapter 1, in the case of WorldCom, CFO Scott Sullivan simply reclassified billions of dollars of WorldCom operating debt to its capital investment accounts. Thus, he shifted a ton of current liabilities, which were making WorldCom less profitable than he (and Wall Street analysts) preferred, by recategorizing these debts as long-term capital expenses, resulting in a substantial improvement on paper of the company's financial performance.

Unfortunately, WorldCom still was obligated to pay the debts—regardless of their classification—which meant that if regulators and Wall Street ever got wind of Sullivan's improper accounting tricks, the company's lenders would probably stop lending and the credit rating agencies would downgrade its debt.

In fact, thanks to the determination and, some would later say, heroism of a WorldCom internal auditor named Cynthia Cooper, that is exactly what happened. Cooper apparently smelled a rat in the WorldCom books and looked into accounting records related to its short-term debt and capital expenditures. What she learned was that Sullivan had indeed improperly reclassified some $3 billion of WorldCom short-term debt. Once she blew the whistle, the company's house of cards began to collapse and it filed for bankruptcy protection on July 21, 2001.

Earlier, it was revealed that WorldCom CEO, Bernie Ebbers had "borrowed" $366 million from the company—with no apparent intention of paying it back.

Ultimately, Ebbers would be held accountable for Sullivan's overambitious attempts to save the company and was rewarded with a 25-year sentence in federal prison. Sullivan, for his part, got five years, as mentioned in Chapter 1.

In 2000, 2001, and 2002, the list of major corporate scandals involving egregious accounting irregularities grew rapidly. Adelphia, Tyco, Global Crossing, even Merrill Lynch were exposed for having cooked their books with reckless abandon. The chaos in corporate finance resulted in the dissolution of the big accounting firm Arthur Andersen after it was charged and convicted of obstruction of justice for destroying records pertinent to key Enron financing deals.

Thanks to Enron, WorldCom, and other headline-grabbing scandals, by 2002, the reputation of Wall Street, big banking, and corporate leadership in general had taken a major bruising. Business school enrollment suddenly plunged as students became turned off by the prospect of building careers in a profession whose prestige had been so severely tarnished.

Most importantly, though, Washington politicians, while ever-beholden to the largesse of the financial industries, realized they had no choice than to somehow placate the public's outrage at the out-of-control greed, and deceit that had come to define formerly respected engines of American industrial power and bastions of financial integrity and propriety.

The major outcome was the Sarbanes-Oxley Act of 2002 and the subsequent debate over its effectiveness—or lack thereof—in deterring and detecting accounting and operational fraud.

For its part, the Obama Administration acted appropriately post-crisis, by introducing the Fraud Enforcement and Recovery Act (FERA) which was ultimately passed without resistance by the Congress and signed into law on May 20, 2009.

In addition to redefining "financial institution" to include all of those amorphous businesses that originate or trade in loans but are not federally regulated or insured, FERA set up a latter day Pecora Commission in the form of the 10-member bipartisan "Financial Crisis Inquiry Commission." Fortunately, in addition to granting the Commission subpoena power and the authority to refer suspect it finds may have committed fraud to the U.S. Attorney General and state attorneys general, FERA lists the specific elements of the crisis that the Commission will be investigating:

- Fraud and abuse in the financial sector
- State and federal regulatory enforcement
- Credit-rating agencies (including reliance on credit ratings by financial institutions, use of credit ratings in financial regulation, use of credit ratings in the securitization markets)

- Lending and securitization practices (including the originate-to-distribute model for extending credit and transferring risk)
- Accounting practices, including mark-to-market and fair-value accounting rules
- Capital requirements and leverage/liquidity regulations
- Affiliations between insured depository institutions and securities, insurance, and other types of nonbanking companies
- Quality (or lack thereof) of due diligence undertaken by financial institutions
- Corporate governance and executive compensation
- Federal housing policy
- Derivatives and other unregulated financial products and practices, including credit default swaps
- Short selling
- The collapse of major financial institutions

The Commission was granted a full-spectrum mandate to figure out how fraud fueled the collapse of the financial markets. But the Commission was granted only 18 months to do its job and it remains to be seen whether its recommendations for reform won't be too little too late.

The same applies to a number of other investigations by government and non-governmental bodies into the role of derivatives in bringing on the financial collapse. While the CDS market exploded by almost 100-fold to $62 trillion in 2007, according to the International Swaps and Derivatives Association, the Obama Administration's call for elimination of the over-the-counter derivatives markets will undoubtedly run into some tough resistance, despite the less-than-enviable reputation that these financial products created for themselves in the early 2000s.

The essential history lesson is that while financial markets will inevitably be tainted by fraud and ethical misconduct in the absence of meaningful regulation, striking the optimal balance between laissez-faire markets and regulatory constraint has to date never been achieved. Arguably, the post-Depression regulatory regime, founded on the theories of market trisegmentation among commercial banking, investment banking, and insurance worked remarkably well until the financial industry lobby finally got President Clinton to cave to their wishes to repeal Glass-Steagall.

Whether the worst financial crash since the 1930s will result in implementation of a regulatory variation on what has proven to work best in stabilizing a crisis-shaken financial system, remains to be seen.

Notes

1. Mary Zey, *Banking on Fraud* (Edison, NJ: Aldine, 1993), 20–24.
2. Stephen M. Rosoff, Henry N. Pontell, and Robert B. Tillman, *Profit without Honor: White-Collar Crime and the Looting of America*, 3rd ed. (Upper Saddle River, NJ: Pearson Prentice Hall, 2004), 231.
3. Ibid.
4. Campbell R. Harvey and Paul Sticht, Duke University, www .duke.edu/~charvey/.
5. Frank Partnoy, *Infectious Greed: How Deceit and Risk Corrupted the Financial Markets* (New York: Henry Holt & Company, 2003), 68.
6. Ibid., 135.
7. Ibid., 50.
8. Ibid., 52.
9. SEC, *In the Matter of Gibson Greetings, Inc., Ward A. Cavanagh, James H. Johnsen*, Administrative Proceeding File No. 3-8866, October 11, 1995, 3.
10. Ibid., 35.
11. Ibid., 47.
12. Ibid., 59.

13. Martha Boersch and Renee Beltranena Bea, attorneys, Jones Day, "The Criminal Implications of Backdating Stock Options," *Metropolitan Corporate Counsel*, August 2006, 8.

14. Partnoy, *Infectious Greed*, 3.

15. Joseph A. Grundfest and Michael A. Perino, Stanford Law School, "Ten Things We Know and Ten Things We Don't Know about the Private Securities Litigation Reform Act of 1995." Joint written testimony given before the Subcommittee on Securities of the Committee on Banking, Housing, and Urban Affairs United States Senate, July 24, 1997.

16. "SEC Brings Enforcement Actions Against Former Top Financial Officers And Managers At CUC International For Massive Financial Fraud at CUC and Cendant Corp. Financial Reporting Case Filed Against Cendant," SEC Press Release, June 14, 2000.

17. SEC enforcement release announcing charges against top CUC and Cendant executives and filing of financial reporting fraud case against Cendant Corp., June 14, 2000, www.sec.gov/news/press/2000-80.txt.

18. Ibid.

19. Partnoy, *Infectious Greed*, 118.

20. "The Bet that Blew Up Wall Street: Steve Kroft on Credit Default Swaps and their Central Role in the Unfolding Economic Crisis," *60 Minutes*, CBS News, October 26, 2008, www.cbsnews.com/stories/2008/10/26/60minutes/main4546199.shtml.

21. Ibid.

22. Gillian Tett, *Fool's Gold* (New York, NY: Free Press, 2009), 46–49.

23. Partnoy, *Infectious Greed*, 376.

24. Ibid., 385.

25. Ambit ERisk, Institutional Financial Risk Consultants, case study, www.erisk.com/Learning/CaseStudies/OrangeCounty.asp.

26. Association of Certified Fraud Examiners, *2008 Report to the Nation on Occupational Fraud and Abuse*, 41.

27. Partnoy, *Infectious Greed*, 321–322.

CHAPTER 4

Reform, Re-Regulation, and the Persistence of Fraud

The Sarbanes-Oxley Act of 2002 (SOX) is widely regarded by both supporters and critics as a legislative watershed in the history of American finance. All agree that the law changed the financial regulatory landscape in a profound way. However not all agree that it did so in an entirely constructive way.

The best thing about SOX is that it required corporate CEOs and CFOs for the first time to attest to the accuracy of their companies' financial statements. In fact they were required to apply their signatures to documents affirming the absence of "material" misstatements in the financial reports.

At first, this caused a bit of panic among C-suite occupants, as they were concerned that with the rash of major corporate scandals still fresh in everyone's mind, they may not know exactly what was contained in their organization's books and records when it came time to sign off on them.

Curiously, despite the attestation requirements of SOX, numerous "material" accounting inaccuracies have come to light since SOX went into effect, and numerous investigations have ensued. Nonetheless, numerous top executives have "gotten away with it," despite compelling evidence of book cooking.

For example, in 2005 Richard Scrushy, the former CEO of the multi-billion-dollar healthcare and rehabilitation company,

HealthSouth, was acquitted on charges of having participated in a $2.7 billion seven-year financial reporting and accounting scandal—the exact type of crime that SOX was designed to deter. While most of the charges against Scrushy related to alleged accounting misconduct *prior* to enactment of SOX, several of the allegations contained in the government's complaint pertain to quarterly financial statements that Scrushy allegedly signed off on *despite* their purported inclusion of materially false statements.

The Scrushy case was considered by the legal and accounting professions to be the first major legal test of SOX and the outcome raised widespread concern about the potential for SOX to either deter or serve as the legal foundation for prosecution of financial statement fraud. (Scrushy ultimately did land in jail on a slew of corruption charges unrelated to his activities at HealthSouth. He was sentenced to six years and 10 months in federal prison.)

Since then, one of the largest U.S. homebuilders, Beazer Homes USA settled a Securities and Exchange Commission (SEC) charge that it had perpetrated a five-year multimillion-dollar fraud involving the manipulation of financial results pertinent to its practice of selling and leasing back homes.[1]

Other financial statement frauds have occurred at such companies as ProQuest, an information technology firm in Ann Arbor, Michigan; Fannie Mae; and even Dell Computer, which admitted to a multiyear practice between 2002 and 2005 of wrongfully manipulating accruals and account balances.[2,3]

Better Antifraud Controls

Despite the remaining questions about how much criminal and civil clout SOX has contributed to deterring and prosecuting financial fraudsters, there is little disagreement about the fact that the law forced publicly traded companies to drastically revamp their systems of internal controls against financial fraud.

The first two years or so following enactment of the law brought with them a chorus of protestation from CFOs about the undue financial and human resources burdens of complying with the controls-related provisions of SOX. But the corporate whining subsided after a while as numerous CEOs and CFOs ultimately began admitting that the investments they had made in implementing SOX had actually bought them new confidence in the integrity and effectiveness of their antifraud controls.

This however, has not come without considerable effort on the part of the corporate and government entities responsible for SOX implementation to clarify and streamline the guidance for compliance.

Twice since the enactment of SOX, the SEC and the Public Company Accounting Oversight Board (PCAOB) have been pressured into revising and refining the rules for compliance. The current sets of compliance rules, contained in SEC guidance, and PCAOB Accounting Standard 5 (AS 5) are now fairly unambiguous about the accounting and control measures with which public companies must conform to be in compliance with SOX. The key points in AS 5, for example, require the company's outside auditors to:

- Understand the flow of transactions related to relevant assertions, including how these transactions are initiated, authorized, processed, and recorded.
- Verify that all points have been identified within the company's processes at which a misstatement—including a misstatement due to fraud—could arise that, individually or in combination with other misstatements, would be material.
- Identify the controls that management has implemented to address these potential misstatements.

- Identify the controls that management has implemented to ensure the prevention or timely detection of unauthorized acquisition, use, or disposition of the company's assets that could result in a misstatement of the financial statements.[4]

In essence, the SEC and PCAOB made a laudable effort to facilitate implementation of antifraud controls over financial reporting. And in general, corporate management expressed little objection to the improvements.

However, several years since the implementation of the new accounting standards, corporate fraud has *not* abated. In assessing the results of a study it conducted on financial statement fraud, the Forensic Advisory Service of Big Four firm Deloitte LLP reported that "Despite stringent historic legislation such as ... the Sarbanes-Oxley Act aimed at combating fraud—and despite enforcement efforts by the Securities and Exchange Commission ("SEC") and the Department of Justice—financial statement fraud remains a public concern."[5]

The Deloitte study points out that the SEC issued 383 Accounting and Auditing Enforcement Releases (AAER) related to financial statement fraud cases between 2000 and 2007. The AAERs encompassed 1,403 distinct fraud schemes. Because there is a significant time lag between the starting date of a fraud scheme and the date of the initial SEC AAER release, it must be noted that not all of the fraud schemes studied began after SOX came into effect. However, by reviewing the AAERs it becomes clear that numerous companies targeted by the SEC allegedly initiated their improper financial reporting prior to SOX enactment, but *continued* it well after the law was in full effect. Others, including Krispy Kreme Doughnuts (2003–2004), First Canadian American Holding Corporation (2002–2004), and Allion Healthcare Inc (2005) were charged with fraudulent financial reporting schemes commencing *after* SOX became law.

The message here, alluded to briefly in the previous chapter, is that while SOX may have succeeded in deterring many companies from cooking their books, it has not by any means solved the problem of accounting fraud in the United States. The widespread fraud associated with the financial meltdown is proof enough of this. However, as the following pages will show, the American "fraud problem" was gathering steam long before the crisis.

Beyond Financial Reporting Fraud

Here's where you get to learn about the nefariousness that goes on day in and day out in the cubicles of business beyond the daunting skyscrapers of Wall Street.

According to the Association of Certified Fraud Examiners (ACFE), financial reporting frauds are by far the most costly of all internally-perpetrated white-collar crimes. However, this category of financial wrongdoing by no means tells the whole story about what is going on in the broader context of corporate crime and by extension, how the evolving "culture of fraud" helped pave the way for the meltdown of 2007–2008.

It is thus important to note that while the controversy continues over how to augment SOX with tougher anti-financial statement fraud regulations, the sharp increase in *other* types of economic crime require urgent regulatory attention as well.

Arguably, mortgage fraud tops the list of such crimes, especially in the context of its direct role in bringing about the financial meltdown of 2007–2008. Amazingly, in fact, many months since the restoration of basic order to the financial markets, mortgage fraud continues to flourish.

But other frauds are on the rise too and must be addressed by legislators, regulators, and senior management (*especially* senior management because that is where the hands-on opportunity to prevent and deter fraud is greatest).

It is true that many of these so-called "occupational frauds" bear little *direct* responsibility for undermining the world financial system in 2007 and 2008. But there is no doubt that in their own way, they contributed to the rapid evolution of the previously discussed fraud culture that in turn provided a psychological backdrop that fomented the "go for broke" risk-taking activities of financial institutions and their attendant questionable sales, marketing, and accounting activities.

In fact, it is not at all far-fetched to conclude that many types of occupational fraud that have grown rapidly in recent years are part of a vicious cycle in which the "bad guys" feel justified in ripping off their employers, their neighbors, or faceless Internet victims because they have in some way been wronged by their employers or by the "system." Consistent with the emergence of the Fraud Diamond, with employee disenfranchisement forming the fourth side of the shape, "the system" has alienated associates and customers by initiating mass layoffs, cutting benefits, eliminating raises or bonuses, and piling on more and more work. More to the point, if top management in any organization sets the tone of "anything goes," there is a virtual guarantee that employees at all subordinate levels will take this as their cue to exploit the organization as well—legally, illegally, or both.

The amply documented escalation of these frauds in recent years is thus further evidence of the growing willingness of employees to cut ethical corners—in the spirit of David Callahan's "Cheating Culture."

It is no coincidence, then, that the rapid growth of these employee frauds paralleled that of the boom in mortgage fraud which the FBI warned about starting in 2004 and which in turn played such a devastating role in perpetuating the cycle of subprime lending, mortgage securitization, overly-aggressive derivatives marketing, and reckless leveraging of credit risk. That is why the many occupational frauds at play in American business today cannot be overlooked. Here is a rundown of the most common ones.

Employee Theft

This is a vast category of criminal conduct encompassing embezzlement, billing schemes, check fraud, travel and entertainment abuse, conflicts of interest, and others.

For starters, there are literally hundreds of permutations of embezzlement that employees can and do engage in. Some of the most popular forms include:

- *Setting up bogus vendors to generate phony invoices that are submitted and subsequently approved for payment by a dishonest procurement or accounts payable manager.* These billing schemes are often more easily perpetrated by insiders than by external fraudsters given the familiarity that the former have with their employers' payments processes.
- *Stealing, forging, altering, and negotiating stolen or intercepted checks.* Checks remain the primary method of business-to-business payments with Automated Clearing House (ACH) credit, ACH debit, corporate purchasing cards, and wire transfers all trailing far behind.

For perspective on the magnitude of the check fraud problem, consider the Association of Financial Professionals' 2008 survey results, which indicate that "Almost all organizations (94 percent) that experienced attempted or actual payments fraud in 2007 were victims of check fraud." There are no statistics comparing the percentage of total check fraud committed by internal and external fraudsters. However, because statistics on fraud in general indicate a predominance of internal perpetrators, it is probably safe to assume the same applies in the case of check fraud. More importantly, the fact that check fraud continues to be an *immensely* costly drain on organizations of all kinds makes it imperative that management invest the time and money necessary to mitigate the risk of victimization.

The schemes described below collectively represent the most common forms of *internal* check fraud that have dogged companies for decades. However, in the context of the financial crisis it is important to keep in mind that check fraud is a moving target, meaning that the "bad guys" are constantly coming up with new ways to perpetrate such crimes. This is one big reason that check fraud has become such a huge cause of losses for banks, corporations, and consumers in recent years.

The following descriptions of check fraud will include frequent mention of *forgery, tampering, altering,* and *counterfeiting.* The check-related crimes they define are all closely related. But they will always have important differences. Until and unless institutional targets and financial regulators get a clear understanding of them, it will be impossible to implement effective internal controls or regulatory deterrents to these costly crimes.

CREATING FORGED CHECKS The Merriam-Webster dictionary defines forgery as "the crime of falsely and fraudulently making or altering a document (as a check)."

Check forgery schemes are perpetrated by employees who lack check-signing authority. The employee steals a company check, usually a blank one, and makes it out to himself or herself or to cash. Or the employee makes it out to a phony vendor or an accomplice and forges the signature of a person in the organization who has authorization to sign legitimate company checks.

This is sometimes easier said than done. It is true that many banks, and certainly most retail outlets that accept checks—such as liquor stores, grocery stores, or other organizations where scrutinizing the details of checks is not a high priority—won't notice if a fraudster has done a poor job of replicating an authorized person's signature.

However, if the fraudster presents a stolen check with a poorly forged signature to his or her employer's bank, the forgery may be detected.

Employees most likely to commit this fraud, according to the ACFE's *Corporate Fraud Handbook*, include anyone with access to blank check stock, or with an internal accomplice who has such access. These typically include accounts payable (AP) staff, other employees with access to blank check stock (including managers), bookkeepers, and office managers.

CHECK INTERCEPTION AND FORGING ENDORSEMENTS Some check fraud perpetrators prefer to steal checks that have already been made out to a legitimate payee, signed, and prepared for mailing or delivery. They intercept the check either before or after it is sealed in an envelope. After stealing the check, they attempt to change the payee (the party to whom the check is made out to) using the "old-fashioned" method—by erasing the existing payee's name and replacing it with their own, either by hand or with a computer. In Exhibit 4.1 you can see how "Julie Smith" was able to do this.

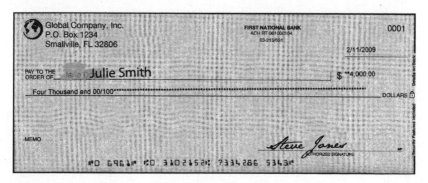

EXHIBIT 4.1 **Example of Check Interception and Forgery**

This form of check fraud is often easy for a bank teller to catch, because the alterations, like the one in the illustration, often are pretty conspicuous. And, of course, if the bank doesn't catch the forgery, there should be a well-trained employee in the organization who catches these frauds by conducting the necessary check reconciliations.

"HIDDEN CHECK" FRAUD   This is a ploy requiring a bit of psychological savvy (often termed "slickness" by jaded antifraud experts) on the part of the fraudster. The criminal—usually an accounts payable or other check-handling employee—submits a pile of prepared checks to an authorized signer for signature. Included among the pile is one check made out to the fraudster, or to a phony vendor or accomplice. The fraudster is able to get the forged check approved because he knows from experience that the signer is extremely busy and rarely looks at the details of the checks before hurriedly signing them.

Making an educated guess that this will result in the bogus check being signed along with all of the rest, the fraudster, in essence, has "psyched out" the signer by exploiting the individual's inattentiveness to the details of the checks, thereby securing a virtually automatic approval through the check-signing process. Once the batch of signed checks is returned to the dishonest employee, he or she simply removes the fraudulent one from the pile and deposits or cashes it.

Too many organizations fail to secure their blank check stock. If an employee with access to blank checks decides to steal one or more, make them out to himself or a friend or relative and forge the signature and endorsement, he may be able to get away with tens of thousands of dollars *or more* without getting caught.

ADDING "GHOST" EMPLOYEES TO THE PAYROLL   Employees at organizations with lax controls who have access to payroll systems and records may be able to add phony names to the payroll and have paychecks deposited into their own accounts.

STEALING RECEIVABLES   Employees in the organization's accounting department who are responsible for receiving and posting payments from customers are known for engaging in so-called lapping schemes. Many of these frauds are similar to Ponzi schemes in that the perpetrators start off by stealing a customer's payment and awaiting receipt of the next customer's payment to post it to the first one's account, and continuing along the same pattern, sometimes pocketing additional incoming funds along the way.

INTERNALLY-PERPETRATED BILLING SCHEMES   You do not have to be a financial whiz or even work in a corporation to begin to see how fraudulent billing of organizations—mostly corporations—has become a favorite of dishonest employees.

According to the ACFE, billing schemes represent the second-most-common fraud, just behind corruption (the technical catch-all for kickbacks, bribery, and bid-rigging schemes).

People have come up with all manner of billing schemes. Among the most damaging are:

- *Shell company schemes.* Topping the list in frequency and cost is perhaps the billing fraudster's favorite: insider creation of shell companies. These are actually not companies at all, but rather businesses in name only. Employees create them with the intention of generating bogus invoices in the "company's" name and submitting them to their employer for payment. These perpetrators are often procurement or accounts payable staffers or higher-ups who have the authority to approve payments. The perpetrators usually set up a bank account in the entity's name, using fraudulent incorporation documents they obtain for as little as $80, depending on which state they are located in. If they are too cheap to spring for the fee and too lazy to fill out the incorporation documents, they may simply create counterfeit papers and use them to open a business bank account. After that, it's a simple matter of cranking out bogus invoices in the "vendor's" name using a basic PC and an inexpensive printer.

But what if an employee isn't in a job with the authority to approve phony invoices and get them routed through the payments process? No problem. Criminals often get around this by entering into a collusive scheme with a co-worker who *does* have the requisite authority. Others generate phony purchase orders for goods or services the company purchases on a regular basis and forge an authorized manager's signature. Then they generate the phony invoices for the shell company and await payment.

- *Phony invoices and other billing schemes.* It is usually easy for financial personnel to verify that payment for an order of goods or supplies was legitimate. Simply comparing the purchase order against the invoice and against the shipping documents, and/or the vendor name against the organization's list of approved vendors is usually sufficient to ascertain the validity of a transaction. (Unfortunately, too many organizations still neglect to enforce this important antifraud control, but the fact remains that the means to prevent these frauds are easy to implement for companies inclined to do so.)

In one remarkable case, Jesse Lopez and his wife, Susanna Garza, were charged with a scheme that resulted in fraud losses in excess of $377,000 for their employer, Marquez Brothers International Inc. Alejandro Cruz, Lopez's co-worker at the San Jose, CA-based cheese distributor, was also arrested for abusing his position as an information technology specialist for the company.

According to the District Attorney's Office in California's Santa Clara County, Cruz was in charge of recommending IT equipment purchases and used his position to recommend buying equipment from a vendor other than the one Marquez Brothers had been regularly using, purportedly to save money.

Specifically, it was alleged that Cruz approached the distributor's vice president in charge of procurement and told her about a new company that could provide the IT equipment at lower cost. According to a statement by Cruz, the Marquez Brothers procurement vice president approved the change in vendor.

The problem was that the new company, Nor-Cal Processing, was owned by Garza. According to a police report, Nor-Cal wasn't even an IT equipment provider, but rather a processing company. Cruz reportedly continued to purchase equipment from the original vendor, intercepted the invoices from that company and gave them to Lopez, who paid them using his personal credit card.

Lopez then gave the original invoices to his wife, who generated new, inflated invoices for the same equipment in the name of Nor-Cal Processing. The difference in cost amounted to just over $377,000, according to the District Attorney's Office.

Cruz allegedly personally delivered the inflated Nor-Cal invoices to the accounts payable department at Marquez Brothers and received the checks made payable to Nor-Cal before delivering them to Lopez, who gave them to his wife for deposit into her business account.

Over a 17-month period, Marquez Brothers paid more than $676,000 to Nor-Cal—more than twice the amount they would have paid using the original vendor.

The embezzlement went unnoticed for a long time because Cruz and Lopez were among the employees authorized to monitor the payments process. However, as in many fraud cases, this one was detected by accident when a Marquez Brothers accounts payable employee stumbled upon receipts from both the regular vendor and Nor-Cal and noticed the markup for the same equipment.[6]

Fortunately, Lopez and Garza were caught thanks to a stroke of luck. But what if a transaction is for some nebulous service such as "advertising" or "maintenance" or "research"? Employees familiar with their companies' payments processes can exploit weaknesses by submitting phony invoices for such services that were never actually provided and initiate a disbursement to the "supplier." In these cases, the supplier might also be a shell company, or it may be an individual "consultant."

Either way, if the perpetrator knows the invoice won't be scrutinized, he or she can get away with this crime until someone gets suspicious, the organization's audit procedures become more focused on fraud, or he or she slips up and leaves a clue that the transactions were false.

■ *"Straw vendor" schemes.* This type of fraud occurs when an employee who is in a position to approve invoices and authorize payments sets up a bogus company and has that company order goods the company actually needs. These schemes occur when goods are ordered from a legitimate vendor and, in turn, are sold to the organization at inflated prices. The invoices are approved by the fraudster. The fraudster may even be able to generate bogus refunds or rebates to the straw vendor, which he or she controls.

■ *Kickbacks involving employees.* Often when we hear about kickbacks, it is in the context of a corruption scheme involving a politician collecting on an illegally awarded public works contract. The high-profile case of Illinois former governor Rod Blagojevich is a classic case of a public servant attempting to obtain a kickback in exchange for a political favor. As we all know, this case was only one among untold thousands that have tarnished American political institutions over the years.

But it might surprise you to know that more than just a few kickback schemes are committed on a smaller scale *every day* by "average" employees—specifically employees responsible for their companies' procurement activities. All it takes is for a dishonest employee to permit a similarly unscrupulous vendor to submit invoices that are inflated, or that indicate quantities that are greater than actual shipment quantities, which in some cases will actually be zero.

After the employee (or a cohort) fraudulently approves the invoice and the vendor receives payment, the vendor "kicks back" a portion of the excess, fraudulently obtained cash.

- *Inventory theft and fraud.* Certain employees are in a unique position to steal physical goods from their employers and to conceal their crimes by falsifying financial records. In a typical inventory theft case (if there is such a thing) an employee with access to physical inventory simply waits until the business is closed, sneaks onto the premises, and steals the materials from storage areas or stockrooms. No paperwork is involved, no documentation falsification is required, and, unless the amount stolen is substantial, the chances of detection are minimal.

A more elaborate scheme involves a procurement or purchasing employee falsifying shipping documentation to make it appear "on paper" as though a delivery of products the company buys in the normal course of business has been made. However, the perpetrator actually has the delivery sent to an accomplice who buys it for a price below actual value and resells it, splitting the proceeds with the insider.

Yet another common variation of this ploy occurs when employees initiate purchases for supplies needed for a legitimate project, but in quantities greater than what is actually needed. Then, after delivery, the excess is physically removed and sold.

■ *Travel and entertainment fraud.* Also known as "T&E" fraud, this is one of the fastest growing and costliest crimes affecting all organizations with employees and executives who travel at their employer's expense.

If you travel on business and have never charged a pay-per-view movie on your hotel bill or claimed reimbursement for taking a friend to dinner, you are probably the only person on the planet with that laudable distinction. It may not sound like a major crime if Bob, who travels extensively for work occasionally treats himself to a $9 bottle of wine which he pays for with cash and adds to his expense report with a receipt that says "Food." But if 1,000 employees in the company do the same thing, say four times a year, the company is cheated out of $36,000 per year.

For perspective on the magnitude of the T&E fraud problem, the ACFE reported that 22.1 percent of all fraud schemes are related to expense reimbursement. That is a staggering statistic when you consider there are thousands of internal frauds going on every day that have nothing to do with T&E. The key lesson is that this is not something to be taken lightly when it comes to the potential for serious fraud losses.

Some employers find out the hard way that they have a hard-core T&E fraudster on their payroll. This is invariably a fundamentally unethical individual who looks for any angle available to cheat on an expense account.

The motives for committing "average" T&E frauds usually boil down to a matter of entitlement. As discussed earlier and in Chapter 1, the Fraud Diamond illustrates the relatively new psychology of entitlement causing employees to feel that because their employer cares little about them, callously cutting back their benefits or bonuses and in other ways demonstrating ambivalence toward those who do the "heavy lifting," taking what they can when they can is justified regardless of its illegality.

In the context of T&E, this mindset is reinforced by the attitude on the part of traveling employees that since they are traveling on company business—an inconvenience and a sacrifice—they are entitled to "a little extra." Here are examples of the common fraudulent schemes that have been uncovered over the years:

- *Falsifying receipts.* Receipts for transportation, hotel, restaurant, and other business travel expenses are easily obtained and "recycled" by employees either by forgery or by alteration. It is all too easy, for example, to alter the date or amount on a receipt before it is faxed or scanned.

- *Making multiple expense claim submissions.* When two or more employees dine together while on the road, they may all submit a claim for reimbursement for their own meals even though the entire bill was paid by a single member of the group. Similar practices often occur with shared taxis, airport shuttle services, and other expenses.

- *Claiming expenses just below the minimum.* If receipts are required for all expenses over $25 for meals, an employee may fraudulently submit undocumented claims for amounts of $24.99 or $24.95.

- *Falsifying automobile mileage expenses.* Inflating the number of miles driven for job-related purposes with their own cars is an easy way for employees to "earn" a few extra dollars.

- *Falsifying approvals.* In organizations with lax internal controls over expense reimbursement, employees may be able to get away with forging a supervisor's signature on the claim forms.

- *Claiming for "Out-of-Policy" expenses.* A dishonest employee may test the waters by submitting a receipt for a personal expense incurred during a business trip, like Bob's bottle of wine. If the expense claim form is complicated, the processor can easily overlook and reimburse an improper expense.

- *Abusing weak T&E antifraud controls.* Improperly established segregation of duties policies for processing T&E claims can enable T&E processors to falsify expense submissions by changing amounts or payees. They may either pocket the unauthorized reimbursement amount themselves, or collude with the actual traveler to "work the system."

External Fraud

This includes vendor rip-offs, customer scams, and credit card/debit card fraud.

As discussed in Chapter 1, outside fraudsters come in many varieties. Among the best known perhaps are identity thieves, check counterfeiters, and dishonest customers. How often have you heard or read about someone—perhaps even a friend or relative—having his identity stolen, with fraudulent credit card charges showing up on his monthly statement, funds drained from checking accounts, and so on?

Or perhaps you have been the victim of a check counterfeiting scam perpetrated by someone who got hold of your bank account number and other private information to enable them to create phony checks looking exactly like yours and using them to withdraw cash from your account or pay bills with funds being debited from your account?

And then there are all of those retail merchants who fall victim to shop lifters, credit card scammers, check forgers, and organized crime gangs.

Cyber-fraud

This growing scourge involves electronically-perpetrated theft of secure data such as customer credit card information, Social Security numbers, driver's license numbers, and other so-called Personal Identifying Information (PII) used in the rapidly growing incidence of identity fraud; online cash theft—either from consumers or businesses or both; cyber-sabotage and industrial espionage.

In August 2008, Albert Gonzalez, also known as the "Al Capone of Cyber Thieves" was finally captured after perpetrating massive Internet-based attacks on major retail chains and credit card processing companies, stealing more than 130 million customer credit card records which resulted in an undetermined amount of identity fraud–related losses to victims all over the world.[7]

When a hacker like Gonzalez breaks into a retail chain's secure database and deploys electronic weaponry to steal thousands of customer credit card records, he can either sell those records on the black market or use them himself to manufacture counterfeit credit cards which he then uses to make fraudulent purchases that get charged to the legitimate cardholder's account. These frauds can go undetected for many months if the victims don't carefully review their monthly credit card statements.

Similarly, stolen PII can be used to fraudulently open new credit card accounts, cell phone accounts, checking accounts, and so on, all of which result in stealing cash or services at the expense of the victim whose PII was stolen.

Unfortunately, there are countless Albert Gonzalezes across the globe. Their dirty work is generating staggering statistics about the number of compromised PII and the incidence of identity theft and fraud. This is yet another glaring example of the "anything goes" mentality that has spread beyond U.S. shores thanks to the worldwide reach of the Internet.

Regulation and Legislation

Fortunately, with regard to identity theft and fraud, the federal government and virtually all 50 states have enacted stringent laws that make it a felony to commit identity theft and fraud. These new measures have helped to put numerous serial identity thieves like Albert Gonzalez behind bars or impose hefty monetary penalties. Additional laws and regulations are in the works to further support law enforcement's fight against identity theft. Yet the fact remains that identity theft and fraud are still among the fastest-growing white-collar crimes in America.

One important new regulation that, after several postponements, was scheduled to go into effect on June 1, 2009, requires all financial institutions to implement programs to detect the red flags of identity theft and fraud.

Banks and all other organizations that extend credit to customers, including medical practices and auto dealers, will be required to monitor their ongoing compliance with the Fair and Accurate Credit Transactions Act (FACTA), in particular the so-called "Red Flags Rule Compliance Program," intended to safeguard consumer data from identity thieves and fraudsters.

The Program calls for training financial institution employees in how to detect, prevent, and mitigate identity theft that can occur as a result of the criminal abuse of customer checking, savings, and credit card accounts as well as installment loans, mortgages, margin accounts, utility accounts, and cell phone accounts.

In short, the Red Flags Rule is designed to force businesses to implement anti–identity theft programs that alert management to the potential illegal use of PII of employees, customers, medical patients, and so on, such as Social Security numbers, driver's license numbers, and medical information.

More Aggressive Action Needed

The bad news is that most of the employee frauds discussed in this chapter continue to grow in frequency and financial impact. As discussed, SOX was designed to indirectly deter many of these crimes, since many of the functions they exploit, such as accounts payable, inventory management, information technology, and so on generate financial reporting data that feed into the organization's consolidated financial records. Unfortunately, organizations have not yet found the proper systems of controls to prevent or deter employees from exploiting opportunities to steal. Nor have legislative or regulatory bodies succeeded in developing rules that would at least place "speed bumps" in the way of dishonest employees and outsiders.

The most recent piece of potentially significant antifraud legislation is the Fraud Enforcement and Recovery Act (FERA) which was discussed in Chapter 3. While certainly no silver bullet in the war on fraud, FERA was certainly a direct product of the financial crisis.

The question for those concerned about meaningful restoration of the country's reputation of financial propriety, integrity, and ethical conduct is whether further restrictions can be put into place—and enforced—to prevent another chain of destructive events such as those that converged in 2006–2008 to bring the financial system to its knees. The challenge will be—as it has been for legislators, regulators, and institutions of all kinds seeking to uphold decent standards of professional conduct—the greed factor. The Gordon Gekko cliché, "greed is good" in the context of defining the positive wealth-creating attributes of a free-market economy may need to be rethought by political and business leaders. If the financial crisis has taught us anything, it is that unfettered greed, while good for those who control the country's financial resources, is not necessarily good for everyone else. As has been shown in true Washington fashion, the job of writing, let alone passing new legal and regulatory ground rules for the financial industry, is easily hamstrung by political gridlock.

Meanwhile, despite the proverbial settling of the dust following the 2007–2008 meltdown, the United States and its major financial allies and counterparts around the world remain locked in an escalating war on fraud. The degree of devastation that the perpetrators can inflict is demonstrated every day in companies, government agencies, and not-for-profit organizations that get ripped off by their ethically comatose employees or attacked from outside by criminals.

As will become clear in the following chapters, the virtual collapse of the financial system in 2007–2008 is undoubtedly the most chilling case in recent memory of how frauds of various types can collectively degrade the ethical and legal standards of financial institutions and outside organizations such as mortgage brokers, rating agencies, and sales representatives on which they depend, to the point that a full-blown system collapse is unstoppable.

Notes

1. SEC Complaint, *In The Matter Of Beazer Homes Inc.,* Order Instituting Cease-And-Desist Proceedings Pursuant to Section 8a of the Securities Act of 1933 and Section 21c of the Securities Exchange Act of 1934, Making Findings, and Imposing a Cease-and-Desist Order, September 24, 2008
2. *SEC v. Federal National Mortgage Association,* Case No. 06-00959 (RBW) (U.S.D.C., D.D.C).
3. *Securities and Exchange Commission vs. Scott Hirth and ProQuest Company now known as Voyager Learning Company,* USDC, 08-cv 13139 (E.D. Mich. 2008).

4. Protiviti, *Guide to the Sarbanes-Oxley Act: Internal Control Reporting Requirements* (December, 2007), 86, www.protiviti.com.
5. Deloitte Forensic Center, *Ten Things about Financial Statement Fraud—Second Edition* (2008), 4.
6. Peter Goldmann, *Detecting and Preventing Fraud in Accounts Payable* (Orlando, FL: International Accounts Payable Professionals, 2009), 24.
7. Siobhan Gorman, "Arrest in Epic Cyber-Swindle," *Wall Street Journal,* August 18, 2009, A1.

CHAPTER 5

Real Estate Bubble and Bust: The Fraud Factor

William K. Black, the former federal housing regulator and author on the Savings and Loans (S&L) crisis who was introduced in Chapter 2 said in connection with the 2007–2008 financial crisis that:

> *The defining element of fraud that distinguishes it from other forms of larceny is* deceit. *Fraud frequently goes undiscovered. Fraud reports understate incidence and are biased. The most competent frauds are least likely to be discovered. Insured depository institutions must file Suspicious Activity Reports (SARs) when they discover credible information of a crime. Many commercial banks and S&Ls, therefore, often filed SARS related to mortgage fraud. Mortgage banking firms were essentially unregulated by the federal government and generally did not file SARs when they found fraud. Investment bankers, in the* four years *during the peak of the epidemic, filed only 36 SARs (For rules on SAR reporting, see page 134.)*[1]

Black goes on to pose the vexing question, "Given the fact that mortgage and investment banks were (allegedly) the principal victims of mortgage fraud, why weren't they the principal SARs filers?"[2]

EXHIBIT 5.1 Mortgage Loan Fraud SARs: Yearly Increases and Percentages of Total SAR Filings

Filing Date Range	Mortgage Loan Fraud SARs	Percentage Increase	Percent of Total SAR Filings
Jul 2002 – Jun 2003	6,401	22%	2%
Jul 2003 – Jun 2004	14,484	126%	4%
Jul 2004 – Jun 2005	21,243	47%	5%
Jul 2005 – Jun 2006	32,329	52%	6%
Jul 2006 – Jun 2007	43,054	33%	7%
Jul 2007 – Jun 2008	62,084	44%	9%
Total	**179,595**		**6%**

Source: Financial Crimes Enforcement Network (FinCEN), *Filing Trends in Mortgage Loan Fraud,* 2008, p. 8.

Black's citation of these statistics is critical in that if you look at the official data on SAR reporting by the government agency responsible for receiving and processing them—the Financial Crimes Enforcement Network, or FinCEN—you would think that banks were on high-alert for cases of suspected mortgage fraud in the years leading up to the 2008 crash. For example, Exhibit 5.1 shows an alarming increase in the number of SARs filed in these years.

Unfortunately, what FinCEN doesn't tell us is that SARs are only a barometer of what *federally insured* financial institutions suspect of being mortgage fraud cases. The data thus provide no indication of the number of cases actually investigated (very few compared to the total SARs filed). Nor, as Black points out, does FinCEN reveal that, "Because insured banks and S&Ls originated only 23 percent of subprime loans in 2005, the most obvious adjustment to using SARs to estimate total subprime mortgage fraud would be to multiply the annual SAR total by five. However, unregulated mortgage lenders made a disproportionate share of the fraudulent loans. The largest mortgage control frauds cause grossly disproportionate losses and represent an enormous percentage of the total incidence of mortgage fraud."[3] Thus, by implication, the majority of mortgage frauds do *not* get reported in SARs.

How Did It Get So Bad?

How the mortgage fraud epidemic got started is up for debate. However, everyone attempting to analyze the makings of the calamity agrees that the unprecedented five-to-six-year boom in housing prices lies at the heart of the problem.

So we must ask ourselves, how did the housing boom get started? Again, no definitive answer exists. However, few would dispute the reality that federal government deregulation of the financial services sector in 1999 played a major role.

That, you may recall, is the year that the Clinton Administration was bamboozled by the powerful banking lobby into repealing the Glass-Steagall Act which since 1934 had separated consumer and retail banking from investment banking. More importantly in retrospect, the law precluded investment banks from directly participating in the mortgage lending business.

However, it did not prohibit Wall Street from extending credit to mortgage lenders. This activity started in earnest in the mid-1980s—around the time Countrywide Financial was starting to become a household name.

By the early 1990s, virtually the entire U.S. financial industry had become proficient and increasingly active in the creation and sale of what soon came to be termed "exotic" mortgages, a rather pejorative euphemism for subprime loans.

In the United States, entities like New Century Financial Corp. and Countrywide, which by the late 1990s became the first- and second-largest mortgage lenders respectively, and other fast-growing start-up lenders were underwriting hundreds of millions of dollars worth of mortgages throughout the country. An increasing portion of them were subprime loans, concentrated mostly in California, but also in other fast-growing markets such as Florida, Nevada, and Georgia.

By this time the housing boom was in full swing. Average single-family home prices spiraled upward from around $100,000 in 1995 to approximately $250,000 in 2005.[4] While this is astonishing on its own, the data for southern California are truly mind-boggling. Between 2000 and their peak in mid-2007, Los Angeles home prices skyrocketed by more than 250 percent.[5]

The disastrous conclusion to that story certainly does not require recounting here. Just ask any of the growing ranks of victims of unscrupulous subprime loan salespeople what happened to them. Their names can be found on the deeds of homes with big "Foreclosure" signs on the front lawn.

And so we are led back to the vexing question of how a housing bubble of such gargantuan proportions evolved. Surely the ground was laid well before the Clintonian deregulation blunder.

In essence, as mentioned above, mega–mortgage lenders like Countrywide, Ameriquest, and New Century were in an all-out charge during the early 1990s to generate as many home loan deals as they possibly could.

For a steady supply of mortgages to fund, they grew to depend heavily on the rapidly expanding population of mortgage brokers. These folks, whose ranks swelled explosively in the 1990s and early 2000s, soon constituted a sizeable subindustry of financial services which became increasingly competitive. In 1991, by which time Countrywide was funding loans from independent brokers by the thousands, there were a total of about 14,000 brokers in the United States. In 2006, as the housing market was in the preliminary stages of utter destruction, there were an estimated 53,000 throughout the United States.[6]

Many members of this group of mortgage-lending "specialists" came from the decimated S&L industry. Others came straight out of college with degrees in business or finance. They were freelancers—working only on commissions earned by bringing new loans to the likes of Countrywide, Washington Mutual, and Wells Fargo. As time went by, more and more nonbank lenders and brokers got into the game. By the end of the 1990s and until 2005, housing prices were on a skyward tear that had the real estate brokerage industry, builders, mortgage lenders, appraisers, brokers, and—most importantly—buyers completely mesmerized. The year-after-year double-digit increases in home values created a financial euphoria in America that no one thought—or was willing to suggest—would ever end.

One of the few who declined to partake of the Kool-Aid was Professor Robert Shiller of Yale University, the foremost expert on financial bubbles and author of the seminal book *Irrational Exuberance,* published in 2005. Shiller presciently wrote that "significant further rises in these markets could lead, eventually, to even more significant declines," and that this might "result in a substantial increase in the rate of personal bankruptcies which could lead to a secondary string of bankruptcies of financial institutions as well," and said that this could result in "another, possibly worldwide, recession."[7]

Of course, why would anyone making barrels of money in the real estate and mortgage financing businesses heed the forecast of a doom-and-gloom academician? Thus, market momentum, fueled by a herd mentality of unfounded over-optimism about housing prices (and low interest rates) pushed those prices ever higher through the early 2000s.

The key to keeping the gravy train moving—and growing—was Wall Street. The big Wall Street banks had, by the mid-1990s, honed in on the mouthwatering opportunities in lending to the growing contingent of small mortgage lenders so they could generate more and more loans, which in turn would be sold to the Wall Street firms which would bundle the loans into packages of collateral to back securities that would then be sold to investors.

These securities were initially structured in the form of collateralized mortgage obligations (CMOs), which were backed by mortgages of creditworthy homeowners and guaranteed by Fannie Mae and Freddie Mac. Prominent economic and financial historian Charles R. Morris notes the following on the genesis and impact of CMOs:

> The CMO was a genuinely important invention and had a profound impact on the mortgage industry. Traditionally, mortgage lenders were one-stop shops—they interviewed applicants, approved the credits, held the mortgages, collected the monthly payments, and managed default workouts and foreclosures. Within a few years of the advent of the CMO, however, the industry decomposed into highly focused subsectors. Mortgage brokers solicited and screened applicants. Thinly capitalized mortgage banks bid for the loans and held them until they had enough to support a CMO. Investment banks designed and marketed the CMO bonds. . . . And since CMOs were so much more attractive to investors, the interest premium, or spread, over Treasuries steadily dropped [which in turn saved homeowners billions of dollars a year in interest cost]. It is a classic illustration of the social contribution of financial innovating.[8]

CMOs, it should be noted, were "invented" in 1983 by First Boston. At the time, reasonable financial market observers and economists voiced no concerns about the benefits or viability of the CMO market. And for good reason. The mortgage financing industry was in effect streamlined by the advent of these securities, as lenders could sell off mortgages to financial firms eager to securitize them and profit from selling them to investors, thereby creating fresh liquidity, which in turn was made available to creditworthy homeowners. As with later variations of CMOs, the original securities were divided into so-called tranches or segments, with the "top" tranches composed of the mortgages of low-risk "prime" borrowers, and lower-level tranches encompassing loans of borrowers with incrementally less stellar credit histories. The bottom tranche eventually came to be known as "toxic waste," but not until several years later when Wall Street began packaging loans of increasing riskiness (more on this shortly).

Unfortunately, the status quo didn't remain static for long. The safe and lucrative markets for CMOs evolved into new more complex—and ultimately riskier—variations. And as with any debt-related security, CMOs were highly sensitive to interest rate fluctuations. So, while Wall Street firms and hedge funds were having a field day trading in the rapidly expanding market for CMOs and other increasingly risky derivatives, they were caught dangerously off-guard when in the spring of 1994, Federal Reserve Board (Fed) Chairman Alan Greenspan raised interest rates by 50 basis points (one-half of a percentage point). This threw the entire CMO market into a tailspin because it left traders questioning the actual value of their CMOs. Ultimately, bankers stopped lending to the hedge funds which held huge positions in CMOs and the CMO market effectively collapsed.

But this was by no means the end of the line for the real estate market. In fact the fun was just beginning.

The 1990s was the decade of the "refi"—when lenders aggressively promoted replacing high-interest-rate mortgages with lower-rate ones and taking out home equity loans to enable homeowners to essentially turn their equity-laden homes into ATM machines. As home prices steadily rose, and interest rates fell, the temptation for borrowers to take advantage of these "free money" deals was irresistible.

Between 1990 and 2000, Gross Domestic Product (GDP) grew at rates of between 2.5 percent and 4.5 percent every year. At the same time, the Prime Rate declined from 11.5 percent in 1989 to 6.0 percent in July of 1992 before fluctuating by 100 to 200 basis points for the rest of the 1990s, but ultimately, resuming a more or less steady downward trend throughout the 2000s.

Thus, by 2001, when interest rates had sunk to 5 percent, the housing boom had shifted into overdrive. The eventual result of course was the massive ballooning of consumer debt, which subsequent to 2008 was assigned a good portion of the blame for the "over-leveraging" of America. That in turn was fingered for the spike in defaults on mortgages, credit card accounts, automobile loans, and other forms of consumer credit. But, at the time, such a disaster was considered a virtual impossibility because the wanton buying fueled a prolonged period of steady economic growth which enabled lenders to keep lending, borrowers to keep borrowing, and businesses to keep profiting. (Since consumer spending makes up as much as two-thirds of total GDP, the more equity homeowners pulled out of the their homes and spent on discretionary items such as vacation homes, home improvement, and gas-guzzling SUVs, the longer the economy continued to expand.) In addition, with housing prices having risen to the point of making homeowners feel rich based on the accumulated equity in their homes, millions decided to trade up to larger, more expensive homes. The trend touched off the boomlet in "McMansions"—homes of 3,000–8,000 square feet—which put homebuilders such as Toll Brothers, KB Homes, and Hovnanian on a construction tear for several highly profitable years.

By the mid-2000s, though, the market for homes of all sizes in virtually all markets had all but evaporated. Owners could not sell into a suddenly glutted market and builders were forced to put new construction plans on hold.

But high-flying Wall Streeters were having way too much fun to let a little thing like a housing glut shut down their party.

To keep the derivatives market growing, big investment banks began pressing lenders to generate more and more mortgages. And that meant only one thing: Lenders had to start offering mortgages to prospective homeowners with less-than-top-rated credit. In other words, they had to find ways to sell subprime loans without running excessive risk of losses if the borrowers defaulted.

As Charles Morris puts it, "By 2003 or so, mortgage lenders were running out of people they could *plausibly* lend to [emphasis added]. Instead of curtailing lending, they spread their nets to vacuum up prospects with little hope of repaying their loans. Subprime lending jumped from an annual volume of $145 billion in 2001 to $625 billion in 2005, more than 20 percent of total issuances."[9]

This brief four-year window was the period when the house of cards that would ultimately collapse in 2007 was being built at a dizzying pace. It wasn't just a matter of lenders extending mortgages to high-risk borrowers; they literally invaded key markets with promotions for loans offering irresistibly low payments to get any borrower they could to take a loan.

Hence the emergence of the infamous "teaser" loans of the late 1990s and early 2000s. Eager to maintain, or preferably enhance, the flow of mortgage closings, mortgage lenders lowered their lending standards, giving increasingly numerous, competitive—and greedy—brokers the opportunity to go after prospective borrowers with dubious or decidedly inadequate means to repay the loans. And go after them they did—with every trick imaginable. . . .

Subprime Mortgages: Licenses to Steal

It must be pointed out that not all subprime mortgages were fraudulent. In plenty of instances, so-called "marginal" borrowers who couldn't qualify for conforming mortgages—mortgages whose prospective borrowers met Fannie Mae standards—due to a blemish or two on their credit record were approved for subprime loans that were offered by honest brokers and lenders. And most made their monthly payments on time without interruption.

Unfortunately, according to Richard Bitner, a former subprime lender, "About three-quarters of all subprime loan applications sent by mortgage brokers to lenders for approval and funding during the heyday of subprime lending were in one form or another misleading, incorrect, or outright fraudulent."[10]

According to Bitner, subprime mortgage deception occurred mainly by:

- Indicating that the borrower will occupy a property when he or she is actually buying it as an investment.
- Falsifying a borrower's employment history by having a friend or relative who owns a business say the person works there.
- Hiding a critical piece of information or not disclosing something about the loan and hoping the lender won't find out.

Within each of these three categories is a long list of specific document falsification ploys aimed at deceiving prospective lending institutions. Several of them are red flags or clues that fraud is being perpetrated (as explained later in this chapter).

Bitner further witnessed the "house of cards" scenario first hand. But he also witnessed the seamier side of the situation. As investment banks bought more and more mortgages from lenders in the 1990s in order to securitize and sell them, they boosted demand for subprime loans, causing lenders to drastically relax the standards for approving mortgages, thereby further fueling more broker fraud in order to generate more commission income from selling the loans.

Bitner says that "While subprime lending fraud did not alone cause the financial system to 'fall off a cliff' in 2008, it substantially accelerated its inexorable slide toward the precipice."[11]

Bitner's assessment underscores the unanswered question of who is to blame for what in the subprime mess. As he and many other industry experts suggest, greedy or obsessively competitive bankers looking to boost profits from securities backed by risky mortgages may have catalyzed the mad dash to a crisis. But they could not have succeeded without the aggressive and widespread—and often blatantly illegal—activities of outside brokers, appraisers, builders, and sales reps. This will become increasingly evident later in this chapter.

Who Is Subprime?

The definition of a subprime borrower is someone with a range of credit risk characteristics including one or more of the following:

- Two or more 30-day delinquencies in the last 12 months, or one or more 60-day delinquencies in the last 24 months.
- Judgment, foreclosure, repossession, or charge-off in the prior 24 months.
- Bankruptcy in the last five years.
- Relatively high default probability as evidenced by, for example, a credit bureau risk score (FICO) of 660 or below (depending on the product/collateral), or other bureau or proprietary scores with an equivalent default probability likelihood.
- Debt service-to-income ratio of 50 percent or greater or otherwise limited ability to cover family living expenses after deducting total debt-service requirements from monthly income.[12]

As mentioned, subprime lending did not start off as the fraud-ridden practice that Richard Bitner describes. In its early years, subprime brokers would seek to secure loans with higher rates than conventional loans and borrowers were delighted to become homeowners, never missing a payment.

But subprime mortgage brokering lost its moral compass in part because the brokers weren't (and still aren't) regulated, and partly because of the growing competition among nonbank unregulated lenders to find more and more borrowers. This created a powerful incentive for banks and mortgage lenders to relax lending standards and for brokers to exploit this to criminal ends.

Critical to appreciating the immensely destructive role that fraud played in the subprime lending business and by extension, the ultimate collapse of the financial system is what William Black refers to as "accounting control frauds." These are situations in which the CEOs of unregulated lenders exploit the institution to defraud customers and shareholders. As Black concludes:

No regulation forced any lender to make a bad loan.... When compensation schemes are perverse . . . [the CEOs] maximize short-term accounting "profits" in order to increase their wealth. Making bad loans, growing rapidly, and extreme leverage maximize "profits." Bad borrowers agree to pay more and it is impossible to grow rapidly via high quality lending. Lending to the uncreditworthy requires the CEO to suborn controls, maximizing "adverse selection." This produced an "epidemic" of mortgage fraud, particularly in the unregulated nonprime sector. The FBI began warning in September 2004 about the mortgage fraud "epidemic." Fraudulent loans cause huge direct losses, but the epidemic also hyper-inflated and extended the housing bubble, and eviscerated trust, causing catastrophic indirect losses. When

*we do not regulate or supervise financial markets we, de
facto, decriminalize control fraud. The regulators are the
cops on the beat against control fraud—and control fraud
causes greater financial losses than all other forms of property
crime combined.*[13]

This assessment is among the most compelling explanations
of how the entire mortgage lending system degenerated into a
feeding frenzy for fraudulent lenders, brokers, appraisers, title
companies, underwriters, and accountants.

It explains how the smorgasbord of fraudulent mortgage
practices (many of them not new to the home financing business, but certainly exploited on an unprecedented scale during
the "bubble period") came to virtually dominate the entire mortgage business.

On October 7, 2004, Chris Swecker, then Assistant Director
Criminal Investigative Division Federal Bureau of Investigation testified before the House Financial Services Subcommittee
on Housing and Community Opportunity that, "If fraudulent
practices become systemic within the mortgage industry and
mortgage fraud is allowed to become unrestrained, it will ultimately place financial institutions at risk and have adverse
effects on the stock market. Investors may lose faith and
require higher returns from mortgage backed securities. This
may result in higher interest rates and fees paid by borrowers
and limit the amount of investment funds available for mortgage
loans."[14]

Swecker noted in the same testimony that the FBI at the time
was concentrating its mortgage fraud investigation resources
on fraud perpetrated by insiders among which he included,
"appraisers, accountants, attorneys, real estate brokers, mortgage underwriters and processors, settlement/title company
employees, mortgage brokers, loan originators and other mortgage professionals engaged in the mortgage industry."[15]

Among the deceptive or fraudulent mortgage lending activities Swecker was referring to are marketing loans designed by increasingly aggressive lenders to enable subprime borrowers to obtain mortgages. These loans—though not necessarily fraudulent in structure, but highly susceptible to abuse—included:

- *Negative amortization loans.* These enabled borrowers to make rock bottom monthly payments that didn't even cover the interest, let alone any of the principal. The unpaid interest and principal would simply be added to the principal at what Morris calls "killer rates." And, Morris adds, unbeknownst to the victims of these deceptive "deals," "gross overcharges for fees and brokerage were buried in the loan principal."[16]

  Often, however, additional frauds were perpetrated on these borrowers by eliminating conventional escrow accounts that would cover property tax payments. Naturally, when brokers conveniently neglected to explain this detail to their "customers," borrowers promptly defaulted on their tax bills, their mortgages, or both.

- *Stated income loans.* These were mortgages that enabled applicants to completely omit details about their income. They could in effect make up any number they wanted to reflect their annual income. Hence the term "liar's loans" which came to describe loans that brokers, lenders, underwriters, and Wall Street firms knew to be completely fraudulent. Making these loans even more attractive for borrowers (and brokers who earned commissions on them) was that they very often required no down payment.

  According to Bitner, when stated income loans were originally introduced in the 1980s, they were intended for borrowers who were self employed and because of their erratic monthly income, needed a mortgage that enabled them to qualify without being able to accurately represent their annual income. However, in those days, lenders required the applicant to have a high credit score and to make a substantial down payment. They also carefully scrutinized the appraisal reports on the homes for which borrowers were seeking financing.

However, in the 1990s and early 2000s, lenders threw these standards out the window. They allowed anyone without a steady paycheck to flagrantly fictionalize their income. They offered 100 percent financing—that is, no down payment—and didn't even require applicants to produce tax returns or pay stubs.

One category of these loans was called "Alt-A" mortgages. They were offered to borrowers with high credit ratings but who were sucked into the trap of believing that home prices would continue rising indefinitely. The loans offered seductively low introductory rates but would reset to market levels after the initial period. They were especially attractive to borrowers because they typically were also stated-income loans, requiring no employment documentation. During the subprime heyday, Alt-As included stated income, stated income/stated asset, or no income/no asset loans that were offered by both prime and subprime lenders. According to an FBI report, this made them very vulnerable to fraud: "BasePoint Analytics, a fraud analysis and consulting service, analyzed loans that were originated between 2002 and 2006; nearly one million Alt-A loans and three million nonprime loans were evaluated. The relative fraud-loss rate of Alt-A loans was more than three times higher than nonprime loans. Losses within Alt-A loans were caused by income misrepresentations, employment frauds, straw buyers, investor-related frauds, and occupancy frauds."[17]

- *Payment option—ARMs*. The option ARM offered the choice of making payments in accordance with traditional amortization or a low introductory payment that didn't even cover interest costs, leaving the borrower deeper in debt each month. When the introductory rate reset to market levels, borrowers typically experienced "payment shock" as they suddenly found themselves facing monthly mortgage bills several hundred dollars higher than they were used to. These loans began defaulting in rapidly rising numbers beginning in 2006 and 2007.

- *The "2/28 loan."* This loan offered a low rate for the first two years that would then jump by as much as six percentage points. Borrowers ideally could clean up their credit and refinance the loan before rates rose. That produced a second windfall for the broker, and triggered thousands of dollars in prepayment penalties for replacing the original loan.

Going for Broke(r)

With so many "goodies" in their bags of tricks, mortgage brokers in the early 2000s went literally crazy scouting out willing borrowers who needed little more than a Social Security number and a checking account to qualify for a mortgage.

If there ever was a formula for legalized fraud, the increased use of these "easy access" loans offered by unregulated lenders was it.

As ex-subprime lender Bitner writes, "In theory, brokers are the best option when shopping for a mortgage loan. With access to dozens of lenders and hundreds of programs, brokers offer a one-stop alternative to applying with multiple lenders."[18]

And indeed, this was pretty much how the "plain vanilla," conforming mortgage market had functioned for decades leading up to the late 1990s. And legitimate brokers continue to provide value for so-called "prime" borrowers seeking the best deal in mortgage markets that have become complex, confusing, and virtually incomprehensible. However, in the subprime industry, the situation was quite different in the short but truly insane years between 2000 and 2006. Bitner puts it this way:

> *It's easy to understand why the lending industry attracts unethical behavior—hundreds of millions of dollars in business are transacted on a daily basis. There are no official estimates, but it's widely believed that lenders lose tens of millions of dollars annually as a result of fraudulent activity. . . . Mortgage fraud is any activity that's intended to deceive or mislead a mortgage lender. . . . These scams often involve multiple parties—brokers, appraisers, and title companies. Even though a thorough quality control review increases the likelihood a fraudulent loan will be identified prior to closing, it's impossible to catch every one. At some point, most subprime lenders were victimized by one of these scams.*[19]

As indicated earlier, many of the subprime loans approved by banks were not technically fraudulent, even though they were approved for borrowers with poor credit histories and therefore were excessively risky. However, as Bitner points out, in the late 1990s and early 2000s, banks didn't care much about a particular borrower's lack of creditworthiness because once the loan was approved it was quickly sold off to a larger financial institution which bundled it with other subprime loans to be collateralized into mortgage-backed securities (MBSs) for sale on the open securities markets.

This practice was not fraudulent—as long as the brokers who were submitting mortgage applications on behalf of subprime borrowers didn't include false or misleading information on those applications.

Therein, however—as the cliché goes—lies the rub. In an astonishing number of instances, they did exactly that to ensure that a loan would be approved even though most lenders had already drastically relaxed approval standards. And in most cases, these unscrupulous brokers acted in concert with equally deceitful accomplices such as:

- Real estate appraisers who, in exchange for a part of the proceeds of the fraud, or just because they feared losing work for not going along, produced often grossly inflated prices of properties being mortgaged
- Dishonest title companies that falsified documents to facilitate the closing on fraudulent loans
- Underwriters who got paid either to approve fraudulent loans or were literally forced to do so by overly aggressive, bonus-hungry bank executives
- Greedy, unethical attorneys who received fees for falsifying mortgage documents
- Corrupt bank employees who were either paid or simply convinced to "look the other way" when mortgage applications containing obviously false and misleading information came across their desks

A notably egregious example of how this and similar broker-initiated frauds can occur was reported by the FBI:

A criminal complaint was filed in the Eastern District of Michigan alleging Rodney Dumas, a mortgage broker, and Derek Walker, president of Fidelity Funding, conspired to obtain fraudulent mortgages by "flipping" properties....

In this scheme, Rodney Dumas (or other conspirators) would buy a run-down property, or a property in foreclosure, for a very low price; often, the properties were completely uninhabitable. Dumas might purchase the property in his own name, or in the name of a company he has established for that purpose, CMB Investments. As quickly as possible, Dumas would resell the property. He would obtain a fraudulent appraisal of the property that grossly inflates its value.

He would then pay an individual with a good credit rating willing to act as a "straw buyer," obtaining a mortgage on the property in the amount of the falsely inflated appraisal and then letting it go into default. If necessary, Dumas and his co-conspirators would supply false employment and bank account documents, and even create false Federal Income Tax Returns, to support the mortgage application of the straw buyer and to persuade the lending institution that the buyer would be able to re-pay the mortgage loan.

On occasion, Derek Walker paid underwriters and others whose job it was to review the mortgage applications to "look the other way" and ignore irregularities. Relying on the series of false representations, the banks approved the mortgages and paid the conspirators the inflated value of the property at closing. Dumas, Walker and their co-conspirators, usually including the straw buyer, would then divide the proceeds of the fraud and the mortgages went into default. The banks were left with significant losses and nearly worthless collateral.

Losses attributed to the fraud conspiracy totaled over $2,500,000.[20]

By the early 2000s, just about anyone who had anything to do with the residential mortgage business had ample opportunity to game the system. Lured by the seemingly endless boom in home prices throughout the country, far too many did. Unfortunately, the carnage left by them not only included countless innocent straw buyer victims whose credit was obliterated but also the livelihoods and careers of tens of thousands of honest banking employees whose employers went bankrupt in the process.

It will take years if not decades to sort out the legal morass that was created by the subprime fraud frenzy. As this book goes to press, hundreds of borrower lawsuits are already in the courts, seeking damages from allegedly dishonest brokers, bank executives, underwriters, attorneys, and others who are charged with a panoply of mortgage-related frauds.

In the next chapter, we'll delve into the specific types of mortgage scams that played such a devastating role in hobbling the global financial system.

Notes

1. William K. Black, "Adam Smith Was Right about Corporate CEOs' Incentives Absent Effective Regulation," *Cato Unbound* (December 4, 2008), www.cato-unbound.org/2008/12/04/william-k-black/adam-smith-was-right-about-corporate-ceo's-incentives-absent-effective-regulation/. (According to FinCEN, a SAR is a form that must be filled out and filed with the government "For any known or suspected violations of federal criminal laws or regulations committed/attempted against or through the institution if it involves or aggregates at least $5,000 in funds or other assets & the bank knows, suspects, or has reason to suspect the funds are:
   - Obtained from illegal activity
   - Intended or conducted to hide or disguise funds or assets derived from illegal activity
   - Designed to evade any reporting requirements of the Bank Secrecy Act (BSA).
2. Ibid.
3. Ibid.
4. Robert J. Shiller, *Irrational Exuberance,* 2nd ed. (Princeton, NJ: Princeton University Press, 2005), xv.
5. Standard & Poor's and Fiserv, *S&P/Case-Shiller Home Price Indices* (January 2009), 7, www2.standardandpoors.com/spf/pdf/index/Case-Shiller_Housing_Whitepaper_YearinReview.pdf.
6. Paul Muolo, and Mathew Padilla, *Chain of Blame: How Wall Street Caused the Mortgage and Credit Crisis* (Hoboken, NJ: John Wiley & Sons, 2008), 66.

7. Robert Shiller, "Challenging the Crowd in Whispers, Not Shouts," *New York Times,* November 1, 2008.

8. Charles R. Morris, *Money, Greed, and Risk: Why Financial Crises and Crashes Happen* (New York: Times Books, 1999), 40.

9. Ibid., 69.

10. Peter Goldmann, "Subprime Fraud: The Real Story," *White-Collar Crime Fighter* newsletter (April 2009), 6.

11. Ibid.

12. Federal Deposit Insurance Corporation, *Interagency Expanded Guidance for Subprime Lending Programs,* www.fdic.gov/news/news/press/2001/pr0901a.html.

13. Black, "Adam Smith Was Right."

14. Statement of Chris Swecker, Assistant Director, Criminal Investigative Division, Federal Bureau of Investigation Before the House Financial Services Subcommittee on Housing and Community Opportunity, October 7, 2004.

15. Ibid.

16. Morris, *Money, Greed, and Risk,* 70.

17. Federal Bureau of Investigation, *2007 Mortgage Fraud Report "Year in Review,"* www.fbi.gov/publications/fraud/mortgage_fraud07.htm.

18. Richard Bitner, *Confessions of a Subprime Mortgage Lender: An Insider's Tale of Greed, Fraud, and Ignorance* (Hoboken, NJ: John Wiley & Sons, 2008), 45.

19. Ibid., 51.

20. Federal Bureau of Investigation, "Seven Charged in Two Separate Mortgage Fraud Schemes," Press release, July 9, 2009, http://detroit.fbi.gov/dojpressrel/pressrel09/de070809.htm.

CHAPTER 6

The Makings of a Meltdown

Although mountains of news, analysis, and discussion have focused on the role of mortgage fraud in the meltdown, it is rare to find detailed information about the *types* of these crimes that were involved. For those in the business, such as the thousands of bank underwriters whose thankless job it was to review and approve the deluge of loan applications pouring in during the heyday of subprime lending, the ease with which these frauds can be perpetrated is no surprise.

With some perspective on the breadth and destructiveness of mortgage fraud, it becomes somewhat easier to understand how this brand of crime exploded into a force of such immense financial devastation that only a massive credit market collapse could break it.

Among the most common subprime fraud-for-profit mortgage schemes are those widely referred to as *straw buyer schemes*. They usually are initiated by dishonest outsiders without the knowledge (at least immediately) of bank employees. However, a bank insider such as a loan officer can also initiate the scheme or collude with a broker to process a fraudulent loan application for the outside collaborator.

Straw buyers are loan applicants who are used by dishonest brokers to obtain home loans but who have no intention of occupying the home being "purchased." Straw buyers are chosen—and compensated—for their good credit rating. They may be active participants in the scheme; they may also be led to believe they are investors, not knowing the true nature of the scheme; or they may be deceived into thinking they are helping people with poor credit to obtain a mortgage they otherwise wouldn't qualify for.

Straw buyers may receive a flat fee for providing use of their credit or a percentage of the sale proceeds. Typically, straw buyers are falsely assured by the broker that the proposed deal is totally legitimate.

If the straw buyer is just a pawn in the scheme, thinking that the purchase is an investment, he may receive a fee from the perpetrator. But any other promises made, such as paying the mortgage or dividing profits from renting the property with the straw buyer, may not be fulfilled, especially if the straw buyer's cooperation was obtained under false pretenses.

In a common scheme, the straw buyer misrepresents on the loan application his intention to live in the home. He enters into contracts specifying the purchase price, the terms of the sale, and other basic contractual elements.

The straw buyer then purchases the property by obtaining a mortgage by filing a more or less legitimate application, except for the representation that he plans to live in the home.

If the straw buyer is a co-conspirator in the scheme, the loan proceeds may be split with him. If not, he will be left high and dry as described above.[1]

In one especially costly conspiracy case, a federal grand jury in Brooklyn, New York charged nine defendants with a mortgage fraud scheme that resulted in losses totaling more than $90 million to now-defunct Washington Mutual Bank (WaMu) and DLJ Mortgage Capital Inc (DLJ), a subsidiary of Credit Suisse.

According to the indictment, Thomas Kontogiannis, John Michael, Elias Apergis, Steven Martini, Nadia Konstantinadou, Stefan Deligiannis, Ted Doumazios, Edward Hogan, and

Jonathan Rubin were charged with conspiracy to commit bank and wire fraud. Kontogiannis and Konstantinadou were also charged with money laundering and money laundering conspiracy.

As detailed in the indictment, the fraud began when, from 2001 to 2003, Kontogiannis, a real estate developer, purchased and subdivided Loring Estates, located in East New York, Brooklyn, as well as Edgewater Development, located in College Point, Queens—all parts of New York City. Hogan and Rubin worked for Kontogiannis as the architect and engineer, respectively. Together, the three obtained permits to construct multi-unit housing at Loring Estates and Edgewater Development.

To finance the projects, the defendants reportedly subdivided the tracts and staged bogus sales of the properties financed by mortgage loans. To perpetrate the mortgage frauds, the defendants allegedly prepared false loan files to create the appearance that the properties were being purchased by creditworthy homeowners. In reality, Kontogiannis recruited numerous straw buyers from among his own family as well as employees of companies he controlled, including his eventual co-defendants, Deligiannis, Hogan, Rubin, and Apergis.

The indictment charges that Martini provided fraudulent appraisals to artificially inflate the price of the properties, even though the buildings had yet to be built or had only fictional addresses. Doumazios meanwhile provided fraudulent title reports and other documentation designed to indicate that the seller, a Kontogiannis-controlled entity, had clear title to convey and that the lender's interest was protected by title insurance.

The loans were initially financed by lenders controlled by Kontogiannis, at least one of which was run by Kontogiannis's nephew, John Michael. Stefan Deligiannis allegedly processed the fraudulent loans, which were subsequently sold to WaMu and DLJ for a total of more than $90 million.

An important detail of the scheme was that Kontogiannis allegedly attempted to conceal the fraudulent sales of the same properties, by changing the addresses of homes located in East New York, Brooklyn to addresses in neighboring Howard Beach, Queens. In addition, Kontogiannis and Konstantinadou are alleged to have had Kontogiannis-controlled companies make monthly payments on the mortgages, in order to prevent the loans from becoming delinquent. However, as usually happens in frauds of this kind, the payments stopped in 2007, with approximately $92 million in principal outstanding.

It would be a stretch to describe this case as "typical" among mortgage fraud incidents. However, in the category of straw buyer schemes, this one is especially notable due to its elaborate nature and the large sum lost by the two well-known banks.

The important lesson is that this and tens of thousands of crimes like it are perpetrated every year. If there is anything typical about this case it is that it was, as mentioned above, remarkably easy to carry out. Fortunately the culprits were caught. In many other instances during the subprime boom, the banks and straw buyers, many of whom were deceived into providing their names and identifying information to the scam artists, weren't so lucky. Throughout the credit craze of the early 2000s, the banks ended up writing off the fraudulent loans and the straw buyers found themselves trying to repair destroyed credit histories when they learned that they had been left "on the hook" for the mortgage payments.

In some cases, fraudulent straw buyer loans (also sometimes referred to as "nominee loans") were (and still are) obtained with the collusive involvement of a bank insider. Alternatively, the outside "party" can be a sham entity or fictitious individual for which the insider has the authority to approve a loan. Either way, the proceeds of the loan end up in a bank account controlled by the "bad guy."

Fortunately, these schemes sometimes run up against regulations that limit the amounts that bank employees can borrow from their employer. For crafty internal mortgage fraudsters, though, this is rarely a deal killer. According to the Federal Financial Institutions Examination Council (FFIEC), "Nominee loans and similar transactions . . . are constructed to circumvent laws, regulations, and institutions' internal limits or internal policies."[2]

In fact in the early 2000s, the bank lending environment to a large extent *encouraged* broker malfeasance of the kind described above. Recall that in the 1990s and early 2000s, large banks developed a prodigious appetite for new loans that they could sell off at juicy profits to investment firms that securitized them, caring little about the *quality* of the underlying mortgages.

In hindsight, it is no surprise that the straw buyer/nominee loan soon took the most vulnerable markets by storm (Nevada, California, Utah, Florida, and others). This was in part because these loans had a "history" in these states, having been used with reckless abandon during the go-go housing years of the 1980s leading up to the savings and loan (S&L) crisis. In that period, radical deregulation of the industry enabled literally anyone, from doctors to dentists to rug salesmen, to become bankers overnight—with no money down. Before long, this merry band of malefactors conjoined in what one group of noted observers termed "a system of pervasive and systemic fraud."[3] And straw buyer loans were among their favorite "products."

Other Fraud-for-Profit Schemes

Thus, many long-time banking analysts agree that because they were used in ways eerily similar to those that helped decimate the S&L industry in the 1980s, these loan schemes contributed mightily to the onset of the 2007–2008 meltdown. These experts further equate the 1999 repeal of the Glass-Steagall Act with the 1980s liberalization of S&L lending rules. Only this time, instead of setting off a Wild West bank buying spree by crooked investors, the 1999 financial market reforms produced powerful incentives for Wall Street to securitize every mortgage they could lay their hands on. This in turn primed the sales pumps at the broker and lender level where the players came to care only about loan *quantity* and not a hoot about whether their "customers" were qualified to make their monthly payments.

In short, subprime mortgage lending in the early 2000s became a sheer numbers game with brokers and lenders caught up in a crazed scramble to find just about anyone who could be turned into a homeowner, regardless of whether their financial numbers demonstrated a capacity to pay off a mortgage.

Greed Grows and Fraud Follows

Following are the other major types of fraud-for-profit schemes whose frequency skyrocketed during the frenzied years of the subprime boom and which, contributed directly to the expansion of the housing bubble and in the end total disaster.

Property Flipping

These schemes have been near the top of the FBI's list of mortgage frauds for years. But they were cited most recently in the Bureau's *2008 Mortgage Fraud Report "The Year in Review"* as "a significant scam identified by both industry and law enforcement agencies. Perpetrators pounced on opportunities born of the distressed housing market, flipping the same property numerous times."[4]

The FBI refers to a property scam in which, typically, a home is purchased using an initial mortgage which may or may not be fraudulent. In the most egregious flipping cases, fraudsters use a straw buyer to purchase the property by submitting fictitious loan application documents to the lending institution. The property is then fraudulently appraised by an unscrupulous appraiser at a substantially higher value. The home is then quickly resold for maximum profit. Often this is a one-time event. But, as the Bureau indicates, in many instances, the same process is initiated again and again by an organized gang of co-conspirators buying and selling the same property to each other at progressively higher prices, and applying for bigger and bigger mortgages each time.

Other appraisal fraud schemes involve inflating the value of a property in order to obtain a second mortgage or to pad the commissions of real estate brokers or agents.[5]

Builder Bailout Schemes

These can involve a straw buyer or a legitimate buyer who is led to believe that he is getting a great deal by being able to buy a new home with no money down. The builder, desperate to sell the property due to an unexpected downturn (or collapse) in the housing market, agrees to a "fire sale" price of, for example, $100,000. What the buyer doesn't know is that the home is worth only $80,000. The builder offers the buyer a $20,000 loan as the down payment and instructs the buyer to tell the bank that he has paid $20,000 to the builder and is seeking an $80,000 loan to conclude the purchase. The lender approves the loan and sends the $80,000 check to the builder. The builder then "forgives" the original $20,000 down payment loan and skips town. The lender soon learns that it is on the hook for a loan for 100 percent of the home value and the buyer may or may not be able to make the payments on the $80,000 mortgage.

In one of the more flagrant instances of builder bailout fraud, the large national home builder, Beazer Homes admitted to a scheme whereby, to enable financially strapped prospective home buyers to obtain mortgages, the company offered "down-payment assistance." This was accomplished by making donations in the amount of the necessary down payment to a local charity, plus a $300 "administration fee." The charity in turn would make a "gift" of the down payment to the home buyer. Both the charity and the home buyer were told that the payment was in fact a gift and did not have to be repaid. However, Beazer recouped its "assistance" funds by simply raising the price of the home, despite having distinctly promised not to.

After being investigated by the federal government, the company agreed to pay $53 million in restitution to defrauded homeowners.

Chunking

This scam comes in several forms but in most, the victim is a gullible investor who is recruited by a fraudster to purchase a residential property, sight-unseen, with no money down. The victim is persuaded that there is no risk because, according to the perpetrator, the property is either currently or soon to be occupied by a tenant whose payments will be made to the "investor" and will be more than adequate to cover the mortgage payments.

In some cases, there is no actual property, or it is a run-down home for which the fraudster has obtained a falsely inflated appraisal to submit along with the victim's mortgage application. In other cases, there is no tenant or never will be one. In yet other instances, the perpetrator agrees to lease back the house or condo with monthly payments that are promised to be adequate to cover the mortgage payments, but he never actually makes a single lease payment.

In *all* of these cases, the trusting "investor" is left with a mortgage on a property that is overvalued and for which there is no income to cover the mortgage payments. Usually, the mortgage goes into default and the fraudsters are long gone with the loan proceeds, leaving the "investor" with a nasty blemish on his credit report for defaulting on the mortgage, and the bank on the hook for the property which it has foreclosed on.[6]

In a somewhat different form of chunking, the fraudster poses as a mortgage broker, or colludes with one. The unwitting "investor" is recruited by promises to take care of everything from obtaining the appraisal, to submitting the mortgage application, to finding a tenant. Unbeknownst to the victim, the perpetrator submits the mortgage application to multiple banks and ultimately, multiple closings occur on the same property. The individual banks have no clue that they are sharing the collateral—that is, the property—with other lenders. The fraudster, who has acted as the "investor's" power of attorney, collects loan proceeds from all of the banks he has duped, pays off the legitimate seller, and pockets the often substantial excess. The "investor" is left with his name on multiple mortgages for which he has neither the means nor the desire to make payments.[7]

Equity Skimming

In these frauds, an individual or group buys one or more single-family homes with mortgages in amounts equal to 80 percent to 90 percent of the property value, with the rest of the purchase amount invested by the buyer(s) as equity. The properties are then rented but the owner/perpetrators fail to make the mortgage payments. They collect rent until they have recouped their equity investment and continue to collect until the mortgage is foreclosed on. Any rental payments the criminals receive in excess of the equity "investment" are proverbial gravy—until the bank forecloses. The lending bank is left holding the bag.

Identity Theft to Obtain or Transact Mortgages

In these schemes, a fraudster files a bogus deed to make it appear that he or she has legitimately acquired the property. In reality, the perpetrator simply steals the actual title or deed to the property of a legitimate owner. The fraudster then obtains a mortgage on the property, takes the money, and defaults on the loan, leaving the legitimate owners with the outstanding debt.[8]

Short Sales

In one variety of short sale fraud, the fraudster recruits a straw buyer to purchase a home with the intent of defaulting on the mortgage. The mortgage is obtained by having a collusive straw buyer submit an application falsely stating that he will be occupying the home.

Subsequent to the sale, no payments are made on the loan which soon ends up in foreclosure. But, just before the bank initiates the foreclosure sale, the straw buyer recommends the perpetrator as a buyer. The perpetrator offers a price substantially below the market value of the home. The bank accepts the offer, closes on the sale. The perpetrator turns around and sells the home to a preselected buyer at the market value and pockets a tidy profit.

Fraud-for-Property Schemes

These frauds are committed by or on behalf of prospective borrowers (often with the help and encouragement of crooked mortgage brokers) who may or may not intend to repay the mortgages. They misrepresent themselves and their financial qualifications in order to secure the mortgage. The most common frauds are committed by individuals who overstate their income, assets, collateral values, or other essential loan qualification factors.

For example, a potential buyer submits an application for an adjustable rate loan containing fictitious income, credit, asset, employment, or appraisal documents (or a combination of these).

During the peak of the subprime mortgage boom, these buyers were "assisted" by dishonest mortgage brokers who encouraged their "clients" to falsify their applications, assuring them that there was nothing inappropriate about doing so because no one would be checking the details. The frenzied proliferation of these "liar's loans" (also ubiquitous in fraud-for-profit scams described earlier) is what caused millions of borrowers to be talked into taking loans that offered low payments at the beginning of the loan term and then adjusted, or "reset" at market rates, thereby often doubling the borrowers' monthly payments and causing them to default.

As with fraud-for-profit scams, the banks are usually the victims. However, as mentioned above, lenders usually sell off these loans, well before they default, to other financial institutions which package them into securities for sale in the financial markets.

The Role (or Not) of Predatory Lending

The term "predatory lending" conjures up notions of long-standing residential real estate and mortgage abuses such as redlining, pushing unsophisticated borrowers to take on more debt than the lender or broker knows they can afford, deceiving homeowners into refinancing their mortgages that will actually result in higher payments and fees, and so on.

However in the boom years of subprime lending, predatory lending came to closely (if not precisely) resemble a variety of decidedly fraudulent brokerage and lending practices that resulted in inordinately high rates of default. Specifically, as one exhaustive study found, predatory loans include those "involving illegal fraud or deception . . . by brokers or lenders. For example, brokers or lenders may procure inflated appraisals or make false promises to refinance loans down the road on better terms."[9]

If this description of predatory lending sounds familiar, it should. It applies to many if not most of the fraudulent stated income, no-documentation, and "teaser" rate subprime loans generated by the crooked brokers, appraisers, underwriters, title insurers, and loan officers whose actions created the makings of the great crash of 2007–2008.

However, when it comes to placing blame on regulators who many Monday morning quarterbacks claimed should have been more aggressive in policing and preventing the fraudulent activities of mortgages lenders, the picture becomes very cloudy.

For example, federally-insured and regulated banks are forbidden to engage in predatory lending practices. However, in typically federal semantic confusion, the definition of "predatory" as distinct from "subprime" in the context of mortgage lending reads as follows:

> . . . it is important to distinguish subprime lending from predatory lending. Subprime lending includes loans to persons who present heightened credit risk because they have experienced problems repaying credit in the past, or because they have only a limited credit history. Loans that serve these borrowers have a legitimate place in the market when they have been responsibly underwritten, priced and administered. Predatory lending, on the other hand, is not limited to one class of borrowers. Signs of predatory lending include the lack of a fair exchange of value or loan pricing that reaches beyond the risk that a borrower represents or other customary standards.[10]

Furthermore, as outlined in the interagency *Expanded Examination Guidance for Subprime Lending Programs,* predatory lending involves at least one, and perhaps all three, of the following elements:

1. *Making unaffordable loans based on the assets of the borrower rather than on the borrower's ability to repay an obligation*
2. *Inducing a borrower to refinance a loan repeatedly in order to charge high points and fees each time the loan is refinanced ("loan flipping")*
3. *Engaging in fraud or deception to conceal the true nature of the loan obligation, or ancillary products, from an unsuspecting or unsophisticated borrower.*[11]

This description of predatory lending—from the Federal Deposit Insurance Corporation (FDIC)—makes it difficult to identify the intended distinction between predatory lending and the widespread sleazy subprime sales tactics that virtually overran the mortgage business leading up to the financial meltdown. However, in fairness to the regulators, this definitional confusion is not entirely their fault. Rather, to a large extent, subprime market participants bear much of the blame. After all, they are the ones who took the original and seemingly legitimate practice of subprime lending and abused the daylights out of it until the two terms became virtually synonymous.

This becomes extremely clear from the preface to the FDIC's characteristics of a subprime borrower listed on page 125, drafted in 2001—well before "subprime" became virtually synonymous with "fraud":

*The term "**subprime**" refers to the credit characteristics of individual borrowers. Subprime borrowers typically have weakened credit histories that include payment delinquencies, and possibly more severe problems such as charge-offs, judgments, and bankruptcies. They may also display reduced repayment capacity as measured by credit scores,* *debt-to-income ratios, or other criteria that may encompass borrowers with incomplete credit histories. Subprime loans are loans to borrowers displaying one or more of these characteristics at the time of origination or purchase. Such loans have a higher risk of default than loans to prime borrowers.*[12]

What does this mean in the context of the financial crisis? If nothing else it implies that state and federal laws and guidelines prohibiting predatory lending were summarily trampled over by the hoard of greedy and unscrupulous brokers, underwriters, and lenders who were hopelessly blinded by the prospects of fat commissions and fees for feeding junk loans to lenders and in turn to Wall Street securitizers.

While regulators have been vilified, scorned, lambasted, and otherwise verbally pummeled for having been asleep at the wheel as the mortgage lending business was being abused by a frenzied crowd of dishonest mortgage "players," it is hard to determine exactly how much blame to place on which regulatory body.

According to the authors of the previously mentioned study on predatory lending:

The principal federal anti-predatory lending law, HOEPA* has strong proscriptions but at best covers the costliest five percent of subprime home loans. Similarly, many states lack strong anti-predatory lending laws. With legal protections against abusive subprime loans that are weak in many states and at the federal level, the absence of meaningful due diligence paves the way for inclusion of predatory loans in securitized loan pools.[13]

---

* The Home Ownership and Equity Protection Act of 1994 (HOEPA) addresses deceptive and unfair practices in home equity lending. It amends the Truth in Lending Act (TILA) and establishes requirements for certain loans with high rates and/or high fees.

The far greater problem with the absence of regulatory intervention during the fast-paced years of subprime/predatory lending abuses was that the major perpetrators of mortgage fraud in these years operated *outside* the limits of federal rules and regulations against abusive lending. In fact, as discussed earlier, this was the primary goal of the brokers, lenders, underwriters, and securitizers: to perpetuate a gravy train of fees, commissions, and securities profits based on a continuous chain of mortgage-related activities which regulators simply couldn't touch.

This is tidily summed up by subprime industry experts, Paul Muolo and Mathew Padilla:

> *The biggest problem with being a federal regulator of banks, thrifts, or credit unions is that these agencies don't necessarily regulate depositories on the front end where the loans are made. Federal regulators working out of Washington dictate rules and regulations as to what kind of loans depositories can originate and hold. By law, savings and loans (S&Ls) are required to have a majority of their on-balance-sheet holdings in home mortgages. Examiners in the regional offices of both the Office of Thrift Supervision (OTS) and the Federal Deposit Insurance Corporation (FDIC) spent their time looking at the quality of assets being held on the books of S&Ls and banks. Alarm bells don't go off until an institution under their control starts reporting losses or write-downs. The predatory/abusive lending case against [major subprime lender] Ameriquest, for example, was brought by 49 state attorneys general. It had nothing at all to do with Washington. Even though Ameriquest received . . . lines of credit from Wall Street firms and banks, it wasn't an FDIC- or OTS-regulated company. . . . The Federal Reserve was in charge of enforcing the Truth in Lending Act legislation, whose lawyerly description is "to protect consumers from unfair or deceptive home mortgage lending and advertising practices." The description is so*

general that it actually gives the Fed more latitude in dealing with dirtbag lenders.[14]

Case Study: Ameriquest

The Ameriquest case to which Muolo and Padilla refer is important in that it represented one of the few in which a major perpetrator of subprime fraud was brought down by determined enforcement bodies. It also serves to illustrate how some of the most brazen subprime abusers helped to foment the unregulated pseudo-industry of fraudulent lending that in turn fueled the "downstream" practices of selling fraudulently generated loans, bundling them, and selling them to Wall Street firms. As described earlier, the latter then made bundles of money by securitizing the loans and hawking the paper to institutional investors who had no clue that they were purchasing super-high-risk "toxic" assets.

How did Ameriquest come to play such a massive role in the demise of the U.S. financial system?

It all started when a former flower shop owner, Roland Arnall decided to go into the S&L business just at the time—1970—when federal regulations governing ownership and lending standards for these institutions were being radically liberalized. Arnall started Long Beach Savings and, according to the well-researched account by Muolo and Padilla, built the bank with reputable business practices and intentions in mind. Unlike the majority of his colleagues in the S&L business of the time, Arnall focused on viable, well-structured, and profitable commercial loans. However, according to Muolo and Padilla, Arnall (who died in 2008 shortly after resigning his position as Ambassador

---

to The Netherlands to which President George W. Bush had nominated him in 2005), became nervous about being in the S&L industry as more and more of the institutions, of which his was one, were shut down by the FDIC for fraud, abuse, and outright plundering. He is reported to have burned his S&L charter in 1994 and started up a small subprime lender called Long Beach Mortgage (LBM) with which he made a substantial profit before selling it to Washington Mutual Bank (WaMu) in 1999.

However, Arnall's penchant for cutting ethical corners became abundantly evident in 1996 when LBM got ensnared in a federal case alleging that it was involved in repeatedly gouging elderly, female, and minority borrowers. Prosecutors accused LBM of allowing independent mortgage brokers and its own employees to systematically charge African-American, female, and other minority borrowers up to 12 percent of the loan amount, which was four times what it charged male Caucasian borrowers. The company ultimately settled the case for $4 million.

This run-in with the law did not hamper Arnall's dogged pursuit of prominence in the subprime lending business. After selling LBM to WaMu (now part of JPMorgan Chase), he reengineered his business under the name Ameriquest Mortgage Company and due to non-compete restrictions with WaMu in the subprime market, initially began selling A-paper (prime-level) mortgages. But it didn't take long for Arnall to grow impatient with the slow growth afforded by this low-margin business. He found a way to circumvent the non-compete clauses of his deal with WaMu by establishing Ameriquest as a retail bank, which was not proscribed by the WaMu non-compete rules.

(continued)

(*continued*)

After this it was all about "sell, sell, sell" at Ameriquest and it was not long before the company had a presence in all 50 states.

Part of the rapid growth at Ameriquest in the early 2000s was, according to Muolo and Padilla, attributable to one of Arnall's key claims to fame: "...by pioneering the use of stated-income and limited-documentation loans, [Arnall] created a whole new class of homeowners who could buy homes without having to prove they actually earned what they stated in their loan applications."[15]

As discussed in Chapter 5, the stated income loan, aka "liar's loan," aka Alt-A loan had higher default rates than any other category of mortgage. Small wonder. In allowing borrowers—often at the instigation of their mortgage brokers—to wildly inflate their actual income, the lenders and underwriters who approved these loans essentially created a massive pool of mortgages which had little if any chance of evading default.

Anatomy of A Subprime Mortgage Fraud

To Ameriquest, which ultimately became the country's largest subprime lender, the "quantity versus quality" business model was gospel. Because the loans would quickly be sold off to Wall Street institutions for securitization and distribution to institutional investors, it mattered little whether the borrower could make the payments or not.

Thus, Ameriquest's loan officers, of which it had untold thousands by the early 2000s, quickly adopted selling tactics that were explicitly deceptive, predatory, fraudulent, or all of the above.

According to the state Attorneys General legal actions referred to by Muolo and Padilla, Ameriquest's mortgage sales reps used brazenly unethical and fraudulent tactics to get mortgage loans approved for borrowers who couldn't afford the payments.

In one of numerous class action lawsuits brought by victims of Ameriquest's illegal subprime lending practices, the following represented what the plaintiffs' attorneys described as "typical defendant wrongful conduct." It is paraphrased as follows from a class action lawsuit by several Ameriquest "customers" filed in 2005:

In early 2002, Nona Knox, an elderly woman who owned a home in East Palo Alto, CA, responded by telephone to an unsolicited advertisement mailed to her by Ameriquest. The mailing piece was designed to appear to be a ready-to-execute contract. Ameriquest made an appointment with Mrs. Knox and sent two men, Richard Valle and another Ameriquest agent, to the Knox home. Mrs. Knox informed Valle that she and her husband wanted to refinance their home to pay off credit cards and a car loan and to obtain cash to remodel their bathroom.

Mrs. Knox showed Valle their then current mortgage terms and said that she wanted to refinance at a fixed rate. To the best recollection of Mrs. Knox, Valle responded, "We can do better," and asked Mrs. Knox and her husband their ages. Mrs. Knox was 66 at the time; Mr. Knox was 79.

Valle filled out the entire loan application for the Knoxes. He did not have Mr. or Mrs. Knox write down any

(continued)

(*continued*)

information. Rather, in response to Valle's questions about the Knoxes' income and assets, Mrs. Knox provided Valle with bank statements, Social Security check stubs, and pension information, which together documented a monthly income of approximately $4,000. The loan application, however, lists the Knoxes' monthly income as $6,800. This false amount was inserted into the mortgage application without the knowledge of Mr. or Mrs. Knox.

Valle also told the Knoxes that the loan would be at "no cost" to them, and he promised that they would receive $20,000 cash back for the bathroom remodeling.

Mrs. Knox asked Valle whether he was offering the best rate. Valle responded, "I'm giving you the lowest possible rate for a person your age."

Valle and the other Ameriquest agent returned to the Knox home shortly thereafter to complete the signing of the mortgage contract. The loan signing took only about one hour, during which Valle did most of the talking. Valle did not give Mrs. Knox an opportunity to read a single page of the loan contract; instead, he flipped through the contract page by page while stating "This is for [purported purpose of the page], sign here." When Mrs. Knox inquired why she and her husband needed to sign blank pages, Valle responded, "You just need to sign these to get things done."

At the signing, the loan contract presented to Mr. and Mrs. Knox by Valle included a Notice of Right to Cancel. This notice was ineffective, however, since Ameriquest failed to fill in both the "signing date" and the "final date to cancel."

Valle did not even leave a copy of the loan contract or any other papers with Mrs. Knox nor did he say anything to her about points, fees, or the insufficiency of income.

Valle did not tell Mr. or Mrs. Knox that the loan contract—which was based on the loan application filled out by Valle—falsely stated that the Knoxes' monthly income was $6,800 and that Mr. Knox was self-employed by the "Knox Music Academy," a fictitious entity purportedly operating at the Knox home address. Mr. and Mrs. Knox did not know that this fictitious income from a fictitious business was included in the loan contract and did not suggest or consent to it. Mr. Knox was not a music teacher of any kind. Indeed, at the time of the loan application and contract signing, Mr. Knox was suffering from terminal cancer and related medical conditions, and was unable to tend to rudimentary activities without the assistance of Mrs. Knox.

Ameriquest did not provide the Knoxes with the final loan documents until after the loan had been approved, at which time Valle returned to the Knox home with a disbursement check. The check was for only $8,000, even though Valle had promised the Knoxes that they would receive $20,000. Valle explained the discrepancy by stating that the Knoxes needed to "pay off more bills."

Unbeknownst to the Knoxes, the loan was "bought down" from 12.5 percent to 8.25 percent at a cost of $14,875, which was added to the loan principal without the knowledge of the Knoxes. The Knoxes also paid $2,726 in closing costs and $1,114.80 for the first month's interest. The Knoxes' total settlement charges were $18,715.80—despite having been told initially that the loan would be at "no cost" to them.[16]

If the above example is typical of the practices used by Ameriquest loan sales reps (and those working for hundreds of other subprime lenders for that matter), it is no surprise that Paul Muolo emphatically credits Iowa Attorney General Tom Miller with bringing down Ameriquest. Miller mobilized state Attorneys General, district attorneys, banking regulators, and assistant attorneys general in a major investigation of Ameriquest's mortgage lending practices. The investigation resulted in a settlement with 49 states under which Ameriquest paid a total of $325 million to borrowers victimized by the company's high-pressure and deceptive sales tactics.

The problem, as will be shown in Chapter 7, is that while Ameriquest is no longer, there were countless numbers of other subprime mortgage originators doing the same thing and numerous varieties of fraud of the type that was allegedly perpetrated by Valle against the Knoxes.

In fact, there was a massive expansion in the number of subprime lending "players" beginning in the late 1990s and carrying straight through to the judgment days of summer and fall, 2007, when subprime lending began its unceremonious demise.

Notes

1. Brad R. Jacobsen and Michael Barnhill, "Drawing the Short Straw: Mortgage Fraud and Straw Buyers," *Utah Bar Journal* (July 16, 2008), http://webster.utahbar.org/barjournal/2008/07/drawing_the_short_straw_mortga.html.

2. Federal Financial Institutions Examination Council, *The Detection, Investigation and Prevention of Insider Loan Fraud: A White Paper* (Arlington, VA: 2002), 2.

3. Kitty Calavita, *Big Money Crime: Fraud and Politics in the Savings and Loan Crisis* (Berkeley: University of California Press, 1999), 19.

4. Federal Bureau of Investigation, *2008 Mortgage Fraud Report* (Washington, DC), www.fbi.gov/publications/fraud/mortgage_ fraud08.htm#9.

5. Ibid.

6. MortgageFraudBlog, "Ten Charged in Florida Chunking Scheme," (March 28, 2006), www.mortgagefraudblog.com/index.php/ weblog/permalink/ten_charged_in_florida_chunking_scheme/.

7. Association of Certified Fraud Examiners, *2009 Fraud Examiners Manual* (Austin, TX: 2009), 1.928.

8. Mortgage Asset Research Institute (MARI), *Understanding Mortgage Fraud,* www.marisolutions.com/mortgage-fraud.asp.

9. Kathleen C. Engel and Patricia A. McCoy, "Turning a Blind Eye: Wall Street Finance of Predatory Lending," *Fordham Law Review* 75 (March 2007): 106.

10. "FDIC's Supervisory Policy on Predatory Lending," January 22, 2007, http://www.fdic.gov/news/news/financial/2007/fil07006a .html.

11. Ibid.

12. FDIC, "Expanded Guidance for Subprime Lending Programs," FDIC, January 31, 2001, www.fdic.gov/news/news/press/2001/ pr0901a.html.

13. Engel and McCoy, "Turning a Blind Eye," 131.

14. Paul Muolo and Mathew Padilla, *Chain of Blame: How Wall Street Caused the Mortgage and Credit Crisis* (Hoboken, NJ: John Wiley & Sons, 2008), 289–290.

15. Ibid., 91–92.

16. Complaint in *Nona Knox, Albert Knox, Maria Torres, Heladio Arellanes and Maria Arellanes on behalf of themselves and those similarly situated v. Ameriquest Mortgage Company, a Delaware Company, Argent Mortgage Company, LLC, a Delaware Limited Liability Company and Does 1–100 inclusive,* Case No. C0500240, U.S. District Court, Northern District of California—San Francisco Division.

CHAPTER 7

Beginning of the End: Death by Derivatives

The mortgage-driven financial frenzy that ultimately spun out of control in 2008 was neatly summarized by one former senior executive of a leading Wall Street investment firm as a product of the virtual total absence of regulation of the investment banking industry. With "no rules governing structuring and trading in derivatives," the executive said, there was no limit to the appetite for mortgages to securitize which the equally unregulated mortgage broker and nonbank lending communities were in turn more than happy to satisfy.

Under this scenario, it is clear that the practice of either knowingly or unknowingly selling fraudulently processed or funded loans to investment banks and other securitizing institutions provided the fuel to create the critical final part of the meltdown equation.

As explained earlier, as the housing boom barreled along in the 1990s and early 2000s, buying and selling derivatives became an essential mechanism for conducting financial business in the United States *and* in global markets. Recall, however, that in the 1990s, credit derivatives were used mainly by major banks to divest themselves of the risk inherent in huge loans to major corporations such as Enron and WorldCom (refer to Chapter 3).

But the explosively expanding mortgage-based derivatives markets of the late 1990s fueled ever-greater demand for new varieties of mortgage loans—an increasing portion of which by necessity were, as explained in Chapter 5, of the subprime variety.

To keep the money river flowing, Wall Street firms had to provide ample low-cost credit to mortgage lenders and aggregators who in turn would fund the subprime mortgages copiously shoveled into the system by the swelling army of greedy brokers, appraisers, title companies, and lenders.

It was a chain of cheating that went unchecked by regulators, law enforcement, investor groups, and consumer advocates for enough years to build a house of cards that should have caused members of all of these groups to grow increasingly nervous as the period of reckoning starting in September of 2007 inexorably approached. The reason it didn't was of course that everyone was clinging to the hope that housing prices would continue to rise, while failing to confront the ugly reality that this was soon to prove impossible.

Playing with Fire

High-risk, high-yield bonds are a lot like lighter fluid used to start a backyard charcoal grill. It helps to speed things along, but if you use too much of it or apply it after the fire is already burning, you run the risk of incinerating your house—or yourself.

In the period 2001–2007, Wall Street chose to play with fire on a massive scale, with collateralized debt obligations (CDOs), collateralized mortgage obligations (CMOs), collateralized bond obligations (CBOs), collateralized loan obligations (CLOs), and credit default swaps (CDSs) representing the accelerants that would eventually ignite into a firestorm that left piles of ashes still being swept up by class action attorneys, government bailout legislators, and uncharacteristically disoriented financial regulators.

Of all these "instruments"—plus a few others like mortgage-backed securities (MBSs) and asset-backed securities (ABSs)—are considered the two main types of so-called *credit derivatives*: CDSs and CDOs.[1] That's because they are securities based on various forms of debt, from mortgages to corporate bonds to credit card debt to, in the case of CDSs, bets based on the chances of some other form of debt defaulting.

As noted in Chapter 3, most of these instruments existed well before the onset of the subprime mortgage meltdown. And indeed, as many sober and seasoned Wall Street observers will tell you, they played a beneficial, perhaps even critical, role in facilitating economic growth by making credit available to institutional borrowers that might not have qualified for some of the more conventional forms of debt instruments.

But the subprime mortgage boom opened the floodgates of mass credit securitization and resulted in a new and exciting financial environment in which, as economic historian Charles Morris writes, "So long as you did the gritty, credit-by-credit documentation work with the rating agencies, you could securitize anything."[2]

Beyond that, as long as no asset bubbles became over-inflated by the deadly herd mentality and ended up bursting, as happened with the housing market in the late 2000s, responsible and productive marketing and trading of collateralized securities was just one of thousands of routine ways of making money on Wall Street.

For example, as Morris summed up the early years of CMO financing, "Mortgage brokers solicited and screened applicants. Thinly capitalized mortgage banks bid for the loans and held them until they had enough to support a CMO. Investment banks designed and marketed the CMO bonds. Servicing specialists managed collections and defaults. Fierce competition led to razor-thin margins at every step."[3]

Very simple. Very straightforward. Very "free market." Though it became a tough business in which to make *big* money, the CMO market helped homeowners tremendously. Because of the intense competition, homeowners in the 1990s saved an estimated $17 billion per year thanks to the popularity of CMOs and the related vigor of the mortgage business.

Chaos out of Order

So how did the U.S. financial markets get from the early days of magical CMOs and other profitable credit derivatives to catalyzing the uncontrollable forces of global economic devastation in the short span of ten years?

The simple answer is deregulation. As mentioned earlier, the 1999 repeal of the Glass-Steagall Act had since the post-Depression, kept the commercial banking industry out of the investment banking business and vice versa and had prohibited companies in both industries from selling insurance products.

In what many Wall Street veterans cite as a classic case of Washington "flying blind" in crafting and enacting financially-related legislation, the 1999 repeal of Glass-Steagall proved ten years later to have been a colossal travesty of law-making.

As they chafed at the regulatory boundaries that Glass-Steagall imposed, by financing mortgage lenders and fine-tuning the art of mortgage securitization, powerful banks, investment firms, and insurance companies steadily intensified their lobbying efforts to finally rid themselves of the irksome regulations prohibiting them from engaging in each other's businesses since the 1930s. Eventually, a presumably well-intentioned but woefully naive Bill Clinton gave in to the wishes of Big Finance and unleashed a free-for-all that immediately gave unconditional permission to financial institutions to turn themselves into the "full-service" centers for retail and commercial banking, investment banking, and insurance that they had for so long yearned to be.

The results included the boom in derivatives markets discussed earlier. But it also provided powerful new fuel for the subprime mortgage market and the credit derivatives products to which subprime-related securities provided seemingly unlimited sustenance. And that is when the fraud element grew out of control and provided the impetus for lending practices that not only violated state and federal laws and regulations, but also catalyzed the cycle of mortgage buying, selling, and securitizing that grew to disastrous proportions.

Recall, for example, that the feeding frenzy of subprime lending that resulted in the epidemic of fraud by brokers, lenders, appraisers, builders, and others formed the foundation—or what some analysts call the "front end"—of the corrupt subprime business. The "back end" was the territory of the Wall Street firms that frolicked in the unregulated environment within which they freely crafted—and aggressively marketed—all manner of bizarre subprime mortgage-backed securities. As has been described some of these "products" were more complex than others, but in general the cycle of huge volumes of mortgage-backed paper being plowed into the markets at breakneck speed seemed to feed on itself.

At the heart of it, of course, was the seemingly endless rise in housing prices. This trend—essentially independent of any other factor in the chaos of the subprime period—was the elixir that sustained the greed-based euphoria that had gripped everyone on the gravy train of subprime lending.

No wonder unbridled avarice became the driving force of the mortgage industry. If you recall from Chapter 1, greed helped to transform the Fraud Triangle into a Fraud Diamond, with the four parts being pressure, opportunity, rationalization, and disenfranchisement.

By the early 2000s, greed of unparalleled proportions came to guide the decision making of some of the world's most powerful and supposedly savvy financial leaders—only to backfire in the form of the greatest financial debacle in 70-something years.

That things could actually get to this terrifying point should have at least crossed the minds of financial industry leaders (as well as legislative and regulatory bigwigs) when the business environment that evolved after 1999 became a full-fledged free-for-all. Large thrift institutions such as Washington Mutual ventured into the investment banking and insurance businesses. Leading money center banks like Citigroup, JPMorgan Chase, and Bank of America quickly dove headlong into the securities brokerage business. Insurance companies like American International Group Inc. (AIG) bought up retail banks and retail banks began competing for a piece of the investment business by selling Individual Retirement Account (IRA) products.

Why was all of this financial cross-fertilization bad? For starters, despite the convenience it offered consumers, the new status quo essentially destroyed the conventional relationship between homeowners and their mortgage lenders. For decades following World War II one of the pillars of U.S. banking greatness was the local S&L, which made a respectable profit by lending money to local residents who wanted to buy homes. Sure, there was competition among S&Ls in local markets, but the mortgage products being sold were more or less plain vanilla: You shopped around for the best 30-year fixed rate mortgage with the lowest interest rate. The bank you chose then held on to the mortgage for as long as your family lived in the home and you made the monthly mortgage payments on time as a matter of habit—not much more intellectually taxing than having the car washed.

S&Ls did well in these years because they only took deposits and made mortgage loans. The bank's management had a strong incentive to lend responsibly, because a default would result in losses and that would reflect badly on the institution, aside from doing damage to its balance sheet.

The advent of CMOs, CDOs, and related derivatives dispatched this orderly financial business model to the annals of history. When mortgage lenders could sell off the loans they had made to homeowners, the risk of default would go with them. Because they had no reason to care anymore whether the homeowner stayed current on the mortgage or defaulted, the banks just recycled the cash received for selling off the loans to make new loans which would in turn be sold off the same way the previous bunch had been and so on and so on.

The buyers of the loans were often "middleman" companies that aggregated the loans and then resold them to Wall Street firms to be securitized as CMOs. The CMOs in turn were sold into special purpose entities and sliced into *tranches* of progressive levels of risk and then marketed to institutional or individual investors based on the level of risk they were seeking for their investment dollars.

Despite its drawbacks, this new era in mortgage financing wasn't *all* bad. It actually achieved what the Clinton Administration had initially intended when it loosened the regulatory constraints on banks and investment banks: It enabled lenders to dilute the risk in mortgages to homeowners who might otherwise not be able to qualify for a conforming loan due to their blemished or nonexistent credit history.

There were plenty of skeptics at the time who predicted in 1999 that trashing Glass-Steagall would lead to precisely the type of financial calamity that erupted a short eight years later. Among them were some pretty heavy hitters such as Nobel Prize winner Joseph Stiglitz, the noted Columbia University professor, along with Senators Barbara Boxer (D-CA), Richard Shelby (R-AL), Russ Feingold (D-WI), and the late Paul Wellstone (D-MN).

Unfortunately, "I told you so" does not the undoing of a financial crisis make.

Anatomy of a Subprime Deal

For a glimpse into the "real world" of subprime securitization, following is an abbreviated description of an actual subprime securitization deal compiled by two senior Federal Reserve Bank (Fed) researchers:

In each of the years 2004 to 2006, New Century Financial Corporation (a now-defunct mortgage lender) was the second largest subprime lender, originating $51.6 billion in mortgage loans during 2006, according to *Inside Mortgage Finance*. Volume grew at a compound annual growth rate of 59 percent between 2000 and 2004. The backbone of this growth was an automated Internet-based loan submission and preapproval system called *FastQual*. According to Moody's, the rating agency, the performance of New Century loans closely tracked that of the industry through the 2005 vintage.

However, the company struggled with early payment defaults in early 2007, failed to meet a call for more collateral on its lines of credit in early March 2007, and ultimately filed for bankruptcy protection on April 2, 2007.

The junior tranches of this securitization were part of the historical downgrade action by the rating agencies during the week of July 9, 2007 that affected almost half of first-lien home equity ABS deals issued in 2006.

As illustrated in Exhibit 7.1, these loans were initially purchased by a subsidiary of Goldman Sachs, which in turn sold the loans to a special purpose vehicle called GSAMP TRUST 2006-NC2. The trust funded the purchase of these loans through the issue of ABSs, which required the filing of a prospectus with the Securities and Exchange Commission (SEC) detailing the transaction. New Century serviced the loans initially, but upon creation

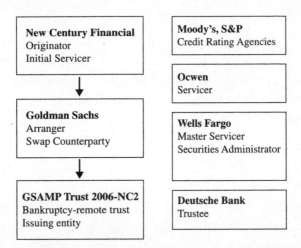

New Century Financial Originator Initial Servicer	Moody's, S&P Credit Rating Agencies
↓	Ocwen Servicer
Goldman Sachs Arranger Swap Counterparty	Wells Fargo Master Servicer Securities Administrator
↓	
GSAMP Trust 2006-NC2 Bankruptcy-remote trust Issuing entity	Deutsche Bank Trustee

EXHIBIT 7.1 Key Institutions Surrounding GSAMP Trust 2006-NC2
Source: Prospectus filed with the SEC of GSAMP 2006-NC2.

of the trust, this business was transferred to Ocwen Loan Servicing, LLC in August 2006 for a fee of 50 basis points (or $4.4 million) per year on a monthly basis.

The master servicer and securities administrator was Wells Fargo, which received a fee of one basis point (or $881,000) per year on a monthly basis. The prospectus includes a list of 26 representations and warranties made by the originator. Some of the items included:

- The absence of any delinquencies or defaults in the pool
- Compliance of the mortgages with federal, state, and local laws
- The presence of title and hazard insurance
- Disclosure of fees and points to the borrower
- A statement that the lender did not encourage or require the borrower to select a higher cost loan product intended for less creditworthy borrowers when they qualified for a more standard loan product[4]

Needless to say at this point, the number of deals like the one above that were created, closed, and marketed during the housing boom of the late 1990s and leading up to 2008 was astronomical. The global market for CDOs ballooned from $300 billion in 1997 to an estimated $2 trillion in 2006.

Where was the fraud in all of this? Essentially it existed at three levels:

Level One: The corporate, or "back end" level, where issuers of CDOs and other derivatives knowingly or unknowingly securitized mortgages and other assets—most notably in the case of subprime loans—that were of lower quality than what investors were ultimately led to believe. As discussed earlier, mortgages of questionable quality (often because of their fraud-ridden origination) were nonetheless in hot demand on the part of Wall Street securities issuers and it is well known that due diligence on the quality of the underlying mortgages was rarely if ever thoroughly conducted during the securitization process.

Also included in this level are bank and investment firm deceptions creating the false impression that the firms' derivatives portfolios were doing well when in fact their derivatives bets were going sour by the billions and causing immense damage to their financial health and that of their investors.

Level Two: The securities rating level, where supposedly independent rating agencies either deliberately or unknowingly inflated the ratings of decidedly high-risk derivatives on behalf of the issuers.

Level Three: The investor level, where prospective buyers of collateralized instruments were deliberately deceived, a la Robert Citron in Orange County, California, into buying derivates they didn't really understand, in large measure because they believed the false promises of sales representatives of "reputable" investment firms that the "products" were very safe.

The Fine Art of Business Deception

Deception by top corporate executives about illegal activity or about the organization's true financial condition in order to conceal poor performance, poor management, or illegal transactions is not new to the world of finance.

Infamous cases such as those of Enron, WorldCom, and Tyco in the early 2000s remain fresh in the minds of business and Wall Street leaders. These illegal financial reporting practices—including derivatives deceptions, self-dealing, and conflicts of interest related to them—have continued even in the aftermath of the enactment of Sarbanes-Oxley (SOX), which was intended to prevent this conduct. In fact, the number of SEC investigations of fraudulent financial reporting increased rapidly between 2003 and 2008.

Insofar as the financial crisis of 2007–2009 is concerned, these corporate financial reporting violations played an indirect but critical role by contributing to the culture of fraud described in detail in Chapter 1.

Importantly, very different varieties of financial deception were at play in bringing about the 2007–2008 crisis.

As mentioned earlier, one involved the credit rating agencies. Intentionally or not (which remains a topic of heated debate), these organizations led investors to believe that many of the complex derivatives being issued based on subprime mortgages were less risky than they actually were.

Thus, it was not only deceptive borrowers and unscrupulous mortgage brokers and appraisers who contributed to the meltdown. The maelstrom of lies and deception that drove the entire U.S. financial system in the mid-to-late 2000s accelerated to the point of no return and the crisis that ensued proved unavoidable.

Secondly, the executive deceptions that came under the legal and regulatory microscope following the financial market meltdown of 2007–2008 represent some of history's most shocking and brazen acts of concealing irresponsible lending practices, fraudulent underwriting, and false statements to investors, rating agencies, federal regulators, and investigators.

Bankers Go with the Flow—Into the Tank

With respect to bank and investment firm executives, the examples of alleged deception are numerous. Among the most noteworthy are the following:

Citigroup

The first example is Citigroup's possible misleading of investors by failing to disclose critical details about troubled mortgage assets it was holding as the financial markets began to collapse in 2007. The SEC began investigating this matter after some of the mortgage-related securities being held by Citigroup were downgraded by one of the rating agencies (something the agencies are, for reasons explained previously, very reluctant to do, but are sometimes forced into).

Shortly thereafter, Citigroup announced quarterly losses in the area of around $10 billion on its subprime-mortgage holdings—an astounding amount that directly contributed to the resignation in November 2007 of then-CEO Charles ("Chuck") Prince.

Similar investigations were initiated by the SEC into Bank of America as well as Countrywide and Merrill Lynch, both of which are now owned by Bank of America.

The Incredible Near-Overnight Bankruptcy of Lehman Brothers

If you refer back to Chapter 1, you'll note that the last CEO of Lehman Brothers, Richard Fuld became so emotionally caught up in the out-of-control competitiveness that had gripped major Wall Street firms in the early 2000s that he ultimately destroyed the firm. He was bent on proving that Lehman was the biggest and smartest firm in the business and to that end, as one former ranking Lehman executive explained it, "Dick bet the farm." By that, the executive, who insisted on anonymity, meant that Fuld, though known as one of the shrewdest and most successful investment bankers in recent memory, became obsessed with the need to establish Lehman as the Number One Wall Street investment bank—at literally all costs.

Because in the early 2000s the biggest profits were earnable by making riskier and riskier bets on the continued upward trend in real estate prices, Fuld went all-out in loading up his firm's portfolio with real estate assets. These included not just subprime mortgage-based assets, but massive commercial assets as well.

As the anonymous former executive explained, because of his out-sized ego, Fuld completely lost touch with reality. He stopped caring about the degree of risk his decisions put Lehman at. He cared not whether the real estate bubble would eventually burst. He only wanted to generate titanic profits that everyone in "the business" would envy him for and which would earn him the coveted distinction of King of Wall Street.

As history now shows, the biggest bets Fuld placed proved fatal and the 164-year-old firm where he had cut his teeth beginning in 1969 crashed and burned, vaporizing more than 24,000 jobs in the process.

It is important to note here that there was no apparent outright fraud in the sense of theft or other illegal monetary gain in

Fuld's actions. Lehman did own two retail banks, one of which, BNC Mortgage LLC was an aggressive subprime lender which may have engaged in some of the "overzealous" mortgage lending practices that many former lenders and brokers are being investigated for.

However, as far as the C-suite at Lehman is concerned, there *was* deception, which as discussed earlier, is inherent in all fraud. Just how much deception and who is responsible for creating it remains to be determined. However, in at least one instance of direct accusations, New Jersey's Attorney General, Anne Milgram, stated in connection with a 125-page civil fraud suit against Lehman, its directors, and its outside auditors: "Lehman's executives kept telling investors its financial position was solid when, in fact, the opposite was true. The state [of New Jersey] bought and held Lehman securities at artificially inflated prices and lost millions."[5]

Perhaps even more incriminating, and equally incredible is Fuld's statement on September 10th—just five days before Lehman filed for bankruptcy. In commenting on the firm's announced plan to spin-off some $30 billion of its massive commercial real estate holdings, Fuld is reported to have said in a conference call with investors on that date that he didn't envision the bank taking any more large writedowns in its commercial real estate portfolio.[6] "The bank believes, given the current market environment, its holdings in the commercial real estate are appropriate," Fuld said. In the same call, he stated that "the employees of this firm are holding wonderfully," an obvious and highly exaggerated attempt to convince the public that all was well at Lehman. What was *not* mentioned was that Lehman was having extreme difficulty raising capital being demanded as collateral by JPMorgan Chase and other institutions that had loaned it money.

This is especially deceptive in light of the description by the anonymous former senior executive of Lehman's commercial real estate exposure. According to the executive, the firm's excessive investments in commercial exposure were the main cause of its ultimate collapse. If that is true, then Fuld's statement on September 10, 2008 could not have been reasonable or reliable. In other words, based on reported events less than a week before its bankruptcy filing, Lehman's iconic CEO outright lied to the public in an attempt to stave off the worst.

Is this fraud? New Jersey's Attorney General certainly thinks so. And countless additional plaintiffs in innumerable legal actions against Fuld, his directors and his former C-suite cohabitants think so. Who, if anyone, will be held accountable for any of these alleged deceptions will remain a matter of prolonged litigation and debate for years to come.

In the end, however, requiring *no* legal proof is the fact that major contributors to Lehman's collapse were unbridled greed and hubris. The demonstrably reckless risk-taking and wholesale abandonment of sound investment banking practices supports the conclusion that the mindset of making money at any cost, which had taken a dangerous foothold up and down Wall Street in the years after 2001, accelerated Wall Street's shedding of ethical standards. By the mid-1990s, according to former Wall Street insiders, lying to investors, analysts, regulators, clients, and prospective clients was a widespread standard operating procedure among Wall Street firms. No doubt, numerous specific incidents of civil or criminal wrongdoing will come to light through the court system as the years pass by.

The (Alleged) Bear Stearns Derivatives Deception

In June 2008 the U.S. Government filed eight criminal charges of conspiracy, securities fraud, and wire fraud against Bear Stearns hedge fund managers, Ralph Cioffi and Matthew Tannin. An additional charge of insider trading was filed against Cioffi. Essentially, the government alleged that Tannin and Cioffi unlawfully deceived their investors by telling them that the funds were doing well, while in reality they were on an irreversible $1.5 billion mayday trajectory.

Though the ultimate collapse of the two funds was not the sole cause of Bear's ultimate demise and fire sale absorption by JPMorgan Chase, it seriously rocked Wall Street and contributed mightily to the emerging reality that the financial system as we knew it was fast approaching a disastrous undoing.

To the considerable surprise of many, Cioffi and Tannin were acquitted in November 2009 of all charges by a jury in Brooklyn Federal Court. The verdict was widely reported as a major defeat for the government in its initial efforts to win criminal convictions of alleged perpetrators of fraud related to the financial crisis.

While the acquittal absolved the two managers of the charges of misleading investors about the health and prospects of the two funds they ran, it did not necessarily mean that key evidence in the case was inaccurate or false. Indeed, while the judge's instructions to the jury were extremely detailed and technical and the "reasonable doubt" standard is tough to meet in criminal cases, the trial revealed hard evidence aplenty in the form of e-mails and other correspondence that painted a quite compelling picture of improper, if not illegal, conduct. In addition, as several jurors stated following the conclusion of the trial, there was a general belief that Cioffi and Tannin had committed wrongdoing, but the government simply didn't present its case strongly enough. "We just weren't one hundred percent convinced," one juror is quoted as saying.

If nothing else, there is no question that the culture at Bear Stearns and the degree of commitment among its senior investment decision makers to high standards of ethical conduct was dubious at best. Prior to the acquittal, Gillian Tett, author of *Fool's Gold,* described the corporate culture at Bear Stearns as one where "employees were highly competitive with one another and 'ate what they killed,' earning bonuses on the revenues they generated."[7]

William Cohan is author of the celebrated 468-page book, *House of Cards* which chronicles in fastidious detail the origins and drama of the Bear Stearns demise. In it, Cohan wrote that after February 2007, when one of the two funds that Cioffi and Tannin had set up lost money for the first time since their arrival on the Bear scene in 2003, "Cioffi told an economist who worked for the hedge funds, 'Don't talk about [the funds' February results] to anyone or I'll shoot you.' "[8]

According to the indictment Cioffi promptly shifted gears after the "I'll shoot you" outburst and the next day held a vodka toast with Tannin and some of the other members of his "team" to celebrate having made it through the tough month of February.[9]

But, as Cohan explains, conditions only worsened in March of 2007. As the funds' excessive exposure to the subprime derivatives markets continued to deteriorate, Cioffi is quoted as having told a colleague, "I'm sick to my stomach over our performance in March."[10] In April, one of the funds' largest investors asked to redeem its investment of $57 million. Shortly thereafter, other investors reportedly also asked for redemptions. In the middle of it all, Cioffi withdrew his own investment of $2 million in the funds and parked it in another Bear fund. Simultaneously, a member of the funds' portfolio management team wrote a report indicating that the CDOs held by the funds (which were heavily geared to subprime-backed securities) were worth "significantly less" than had earlier been believed. Three days later, Tannin urged Cioffi in an e-mail to close the funds. In the e-mail, produced by the government during the trial, Cioffi wrote that "If we believe the [CDOs report is] anywhere close to accurate I think we should close the funds now. The reason for this is that if [the CDO report] is correct then the entire subprime market is toast.... If AAA bonds are systematically downgraded then there is simply no way for us to make money—ever."[11]

Remarkably—or perhaps *not* so remarkably in light of some of the events and behaviors discussed in this book thus far—Tannin allegedly told investors during a conference call on April 25th that "... from a structural point of view, from an asset point of view ... we're very comfortable with exactly where we are. . . . [The] structure of the fund has performed exactly the way it was designed to perform."[12]

Cioffi is alleged to have chimed in on the conference call with a completely fictitious account of the redemption activity at the funds, notably neglecting to mention that he had pulled his own money out or that one of the funds' biggest investors had asked to redeem a $57 million position in the funds.

Whether the additional lies that the government claims were told to both Bear insiders and fund investors leading up to the June collapse of the funds were actually told, may never be known for certain. However, it is chillingly clear that after investors were informed that they could no longer redeem their investments in the funds, it was declared that both funds had lost 100 percent of their value, resulting in a total hit to investors of about $1.5 billion.

Cohan, in a *New York Times* op-ed article published the day after the Tannin-Cioffi acquittals, chalked up the surprising verdict to botched lawyering by the government prosecutors. "In short, the prosecution blew it," wrote Cohan. He went on to explain the government's overreliance on the "snippets" of the incriminating e-mails which in their entirety appeared surprisingly ambiguous.

In portraying the prosecution's "misjudgments" as "doubly vexing," Cohan pointed to its failure to make use of other, harder evidence, including compelling testimony about key documents from one former Bear Stearns manager, which constituted what

Cohan described as having been "as close to a smoking gun as the prosecutors could have hoped for."[13]

While the government's case against the two managers lets them off the hook on criminal charges, an SEC civil complaint is still in play, as is one filed in October 2008 by Bank of America alleging similar deceptions on the part of the hedge fund duo.

The SEC complaint was filed at the same time as the criminal indictment, and included essentially the same allegation as those contained in the criminal indictment, *as well as* allegations about blatant lies about the funds' condition to two banks that Cioffi and Tannin were seeking loans from in the final months of the funds' existence.

The SEC told reporters in response to the acquittals that it will continue to pursue its civil case.

It is generally much easier to prove civil violations than criminal charges since the "reasonable doubt" standard does not apply. Instead, the prosecution in a civil case must simply demonstrate a "preponderance of evidence" in support of the charges. This, as one former federal prosecutor explains, essentially reduces the burden of proof from 99 percent in the case of reasonable doubt to 51 percent in that of preponderance of evidence.

As for Bear Stearns itself, it was only a matter of months before the ignominious end came to the 85-year-old firm. By early 2008, investor confidence in the venerated firm had eroded beyond repair and the only question remaining was how to dispose of the firm's existing assets. Ultimately the Federal Reserve approved a bailout loan to JPMorgan Chase which essentially forced Morgan to acquire what remained of Bear Stearns. After heated debate the takeover was finalized in late May at a price of $10 per share of Bear Stearns. Less than a year earlier, Bear Stearns shares had traded at $159.

The critical factor in the Bear Stearns case is that unlike Lehman, Bear Stearns destroyed itself by way of fraud and misrepresentation allegedly committed by senior investment managers. Yet, several parallels with the Lehman collapse exist in the almost pathological behavior displayed by Fuld in the case of Lehman and Cioffi and Tannin in the case of Bear. These are:

- All three had extreme delusions of financial and personal grandeur
- All were bent on dramatic, perhaps history-making success at the expense of prudent and responsible risk management
- All three were convinced that the rising housing market would provide their high-risk subprime bets with fantastic jackpots
- All three were so removed from the realities of the dangerous repercussions of their actions that they saw no wrong in lying to investors and colleagues about the condition of their respective firms' (or funds') financial performance

The History-Making Collapse of Washington Mutual

Washington Mutual or WaMu, as it was affectionately called until its late-September 2008 demise, was for decades one of the country's largest home mortgage lenders. It racked up huge profits through the 1980s and 1990s as its aggressive home mortgage operation pressed into more and more local markets, ultimately becoming active in nearly every state and giving Countrywide a fast-paced run for its money.

Not until late 2008 did the truth about WaMu's real financial condition and its fraud-fueled slide toward failure start coming to light.

The real story of WaMu's collapse appears in a 400-plus page federal class action complaint against WaMu and its former CEO, Kerry Killinger, in which numerous former employees offer gory details about highly questionable—allegedly fraudulent—lending practices, as well as alleged securities fraud.

In one exceptionally vivid account, a former WaMu employee explained how the illegal practice of inflating appraised values of homes whose prospective buyers were applying to WaMu for mortgages was a common practice among appraisers working for WaMu. The experience of this particular "Confidential Witness" (CW)—one of 89 former WaMu employees and others who, on condition that their names not be revealed during the case proceedings, provided first-hand accounts of their experiences to the class action attorneys—was described in the filing as follows:

> ... *in-house appraisers received kickbacks from loan consultants to "hit" value on appraisals. Despite CW 25's complaints to management about the appraisal process at WaMu, WaMu management did nothing to change the situation. Indeed, CW 25's job was threatened on many occasions in response to CW 25's complaints of appraisal corruption.*
>
> *CW 31 who was a contract appraiser with eAppraiseIT after leaving WaMu as an in-house appraiser, also confirmed that WaMu pressured appraisers to inflate appraisal values.*
>
> *Specifically, CW 31 stated that WaMu dictated appraisal values that it needed to satisfy the [Loan-to-Value] ratios it desired. CW 31 explained that WaMu pressured the third-party appraisers by (i) badgering them to meet the Company's desired appraisal values, and (ii) ceasing to hire appraisers who did not bring in the inflated appraisal value that WaMu desired.*[14]

After several quarters of billion-dollar losses, Wamu's balance sheet showed that the percentage of non-performing assets (mostly subprime residential home loans) had tripled between the second quarter of 2007 and the same period of 2008.

Meanwhile, WaMu CEO Killinger told investors a mere five months before WaMu went bankrupt and upon announcing a quarterly loss of $1.4 billion that the bank "has the capital, the passion, the commitment to . . . get through this. We're going to have terrific days ahead of us. I just want people to calm down, have a little faith."

The rest, as the cliché goes, is history. WaMu filed for bankruptcy on September 26th, 2008 and its assets were seized by the Federal Deposit Insurance Corporation (FDIC) and sold for pennies on the dollar to JPMorgan Chase.

The Countrywide Debacle

Though the subprime debacle lies at the heart of the collapses of WaMu and Countrywide, the calamitous implosions of the two huge institutions are different in many ways. For starters, they were completely different kinds of financial institutions: WaMu was a retail banking behemoth with thousands of branches across the country. Countrywide was what is known as a non-depository mortgage lender, meaning that it didn't have the immense pool of retail customer deposits to turn around and lend to home buyers. Instead, it borrowed from the large Wall Street firms at favorable rates and used *those* funds to make loans to mortgage borrowers (many of them subprime customers).

However, this is where the differences give way to parallels. Both institutions ultimately failed due to the same type of out-of-control risk-taking by their respective CEOs. And both pursued ultra-aggressive, often legally questionable, marketing of mortgages that their customers couldn't afford.

As for Countrywide cofounder and CEO Angelo Mozilo, who rose from modest means to head the largest mortgage lender in the United States, he became another tragic figure in the financial crisis drama. Like Lehman's Richard Fuld, Mozilo's lethal mix of egotism, hubris, greed, and obsession helped to perpetuate both the 2008 meltdown *and* his own self-destruction.

Other senior players in the same general category include former Merrill Lynch CEO, Stanley O'Neal and Citigroup CEO, Charles Prince.

Hard Money

Paul Muolo and Mathew Padilla in their book, *Chain of Blame*, refer to "hard money" as funds loaned to high-risk borrowers such as subprime mortgage applicants. Because the lender is taking a higher risk than "soft money" lenders like traditional S&Ls, which lend based on the quality of the borrowers' credit, hard money lenders expect to be rewarded with higher returns. That is exactly what they get when providing loans to subprime borrowers at rates substantially higher than a borrower with a pristine credit history would be offered.

Angelo Mozilo of Countrywide may thus be described as the granddaddy of hard money lending. He was the one who saw an immense opportunity when S&Ls were dropping like flies in the 1980s due initially to grossly misconceived regulation and then to a wildfire of fraud perpetrated by the likes of Charles Keating and thousands of smaller fry who purchased S&Ls with no money down and plundered them into the ground.

One of the by-products of the S&L debacle was the laying off of tens of thousands of highly qualified S&L mortgage loan officers. Mozilo looked at the costs associated with paying full-time loan officers at his retail outlets and compared those costs with what he could pay independent, "freelance" loan reps, which was usually 1 percent of the face value of a loan closed by the officer. The comparison was a proverbial no-brainer. If a freelance loan representative didn't sell any mortgages, he or she simply didn't get paid. If he did, he'd get the 1 percent commission and Countrywide would make money on the cash flow from the loan, or collect juicy fees for servicing the loan after selling it off to Freddie Mac or Fannie Mae or a non–Government Sponsored Enterprise (GSE) third party which would bundle it along with other loans into CDOs and peddle the securities to large investors.

Thus Countrywide gradually built a veritable army of over 40,000 independent loan sales reps, some calling themselves loan officers, others going under the title of "mortgage broker," but in the end all of them working for themselves rather than for a particular financial institution.

This strategy catapulted Countrywide into the big times. The major Wall Street firms soon began to think of Countrywide as a cash machine and clamored to lend it money that would fuel the growth of its mortgage loan operations. For the investment houses, this was a proverbial double whammy. Not only did they collect interest on the loans to Countrywide, they started buying large numbers of mortgages *from* Countrywide which they could package into collateralized securities for sale to their large institutional clients.

By the early 2000s, Countrywide had also become a major securitizer of subprime loans itself, thus competing with the Wall Street giants. But the big investment firms weren't too concerned because they still had plenty of other sources of subprime mortgages such as Ameriquest, Household Finance, New Century, and Option One.

As Muolo and Padilla write, "In 1991 . . . Countrywide reached a milestone, one it happily added to its growing corporate history in its museum lobby: It was now the largest residential lender in the United States. It reached that milestone for two chief reasons: It was picking up tons of new business because hundreds of S&Ls—especially in California—had failed. The other reason? It was now the largest originator of home mortgages using loan brokers."[15]

There was only one problem with this seemingly golden formula for making a killing in the residential mortgage business:

Independent mortgage brokers were completely unregulated. They could use virtually any sales and marketing tactics they wanted to generate business. And as Countrywide and its competitors came to rely more and more on these independent mini mortgage machines, the "ABC" (Always Be Closing) pressure was rapidly mounting.

Apparently, however, no one in the regulatory, legislative, or mortgage industry communities stopped to ask the question: What do you get when you have an independent broker, pressured to close business or greedy to close *more* business (or both) and a regulatory free-for-all? The disturbing answer would of course have been: A virtual license to steal.

Brokers began pursuing prospective subprime borrowers as if their next meal depended on them because the standard 1 percent commission on so-called "A-paper" prime mortgages didn't apply to those deals. Lenders instead were happy to pay much more to bring on a loan with an interest rate that was in the double digits—regardless of the borrower's level of creditworthiness.

Brokers lied up and down to prospective borrowers, telling them what they wanted to hear about how they just had to fill out the loan application in "a certain way" to qualify for the loan. When so-called "exotic" mortgage products came on the market, such as Option ARMs, stated income loans, limited-documentation loans, and a slew of other deceptive products like them, the brokers' job of selling to unqualified customers became a feeding frenzy, albeit a shady one.

Muolo and Padilla sum it up like this:

By paying a retail loan officer (LO) a commission to bring in mortgages, a lender walks a tightrope: The bonus money spurs the LO to produce, which is great for both the company and the LO. But the incentive money has the potential to corrupt the process, because it offers cash rewards for volume. It stands to reason that when you have thousands of salespeople peddling loans in 50 states, somewhere along the line LOs will jam loans through the system regardless of the borrower's ability to repay. When a company makes a loan without caring about being repaid (it earns points and fees on the mortgages before selling them to an investor in the secondary market), this is often referred to as "predatory lending."[16]

And it was predatory lending and comparably questionable mortgage selling tactics that in the short period between the mid-1990s and just 10 or 11 years later formed the incredibly shaky foundation of fraudulently generated and fundamentally unviable subprime loans upon which Wall Street created its own mega market of mortgage-backed derivatives of dubious quality. The result was a financial house of cards that reached immense proportions before spontaneously collapsing as soon as residential home prices started to slide beginning in 2006.

Can Countrywide be labeled a perpetrator of mortgage fraud? If the question pertains specifically to whether Countrywide engaged in predatory lending, the answer is a definitive *yes*. And engage it did.

In the largest predatory lending lawsuit in U.S. history, Countrywide was sued in April, 2008 by over 30 state attorneys general for predatory lending. Under the Bank of America umbrella, the bank eventually agreed to pay $8.4 billion to borrowers to modify their mortgages, cover moving expenses in cases where foreclosure has occurred as well as other costs related to remediating the fraudulent lending practices it engaged in. Approximately 400,000 Countrywide borrowers were beneficiaries of the settlement.

Beyond the predatory lending issue, the answer to the question of Countrywide's culpability for widespread mortgage fraud remains up to the legal system, now saddled with countless other class action lawsuits by customers who lost their Countrywide-financed homes, and to the criminal and civil investigative agencies that may or may not try to build cases of wrongdoing against the company.

Two things that are not subject to doubt: First, Mozilo, in his uncontrollable zeal to grow Countrywide *no matter what,* ended up dooming the company by originating mountains of "toxic" mortgages (as much as $150 billion worth between 2004 and 2007 alone) that turned sour as soon as home prices tanked. And second, Angelo Mozilo's reputation for building the greatest mortgage lender in American history is tarnished forever.

In 2008 and 2009, the SEC filed civil charges against Mozilo. In the highest-profile government legal action against a chief executive related to the financial crisis, the SEC charged Mozilo with profiting to the tune of $139 million through insider-trading in Countrywide stock and *alleged failure to disclose material information to shareholders.* Specifically, in addition to the insider-trading charges, Mozilo, along with former Countrywide president, David Sambol and former CFO, Eric Sieracki, were charged with misleading investors about the seriousness of risks inherent in many of its aggressive subprime lending practices and actually told investors between 2005 and 2007 that it was primarily involved in lending to prime mortgage borrowers and had, according to the SEC complaint, "avoided the excesses of its competitors."[17]

Meanwhile, according to the SEC complaint, Mozilo told colleagues inside Countrywide that he was very concerned about the riskiness of many of its mortgage products, particularly its Pay-Option ARM loans (adjustable rate loans that provide the borrower with various repayment options). So concerned was Mozilo about the plunging value of these mortgages that, according to the SEC complaint, he actually recommended to associates that the company sell its entire portfolio of these loans.[18]

The Scourge of Insider Trading

Insider trading (buying and selling stocks on the strength of information available only to company or investment firm insiders, and *not* to the investing public) as Mozilo is accused of having done, has been against the law since enactment of the Securities Exchange Act of 1934. The Act prohibits "short-swing profits (from any purchases and sales within any six month period) made by corporate directors, officers, or stockholders owning more than 10 percent of a firm's shares."

The rule was implemented to prevent insiders, who have privileged access to material company information, from taking advantage of information for the purpose of making short-term profits. For example, if an officer buys 100 shares at $5 in January and sells these same shares in February for $6, he would have made a profit of $100. Because the shares were bought and sold within a six-month period, the officer would have to return the $100 to the company under the short-swing profit rule.[19]

The 1934 Act also makes it illegal "to use or employ, in connection with the purchase or sale of any security registered on a national securities exchange or any security not so registered, any manipulative or deceptive device or contrivance in contravention of such rules and regulations as the [SEC] may prescribe."[20]

However, criminalization of insider trading was much more clearly codified in the Insider Trading Sanctions Act (ITSA) of 1984, which gave the SEC the ability to request courts to impose monetary penalties on violators of the insider trading laws. Further toughening came with the Insider Trading and Securities Fraud Act of 1988 which, in short, makes it clear that a penalty can be imposed against "tippers" of material nonpublic information and authorized the SEC to pay up to 10 percent of fines to informers as bounty in certain cases.[21]

Unfortunately, history tells us that these statutory and regulatory deterrents to insider trading have not stopped dishonest financial institution managers from making illegal securities trades based on privileged information.

In fact, many of the criminal charges against Michael Milken and Ivan Boesky involved incidents of insider trading, mainly in connection with the numerous junk bond-financed takeover deals that Milken and his team engineered. (Thanks to successful plea bargaining, Milken was actually never *convicted* of illegal insider trading though the evidence against him overwhelmingly pointed to repeated incidents of such activity).

More recently, many of the high-profile corporate fraud cases such as Enron, WorldCom, Deutsche Bank, and others have had insider trading violations associated with them. And the widely-publicized late-2009 announcement of insider trading charges against the top executives of Galleon Management, which the FBI called the largest hedge fund insider trading case in history, suggests that such criminal activity remains a serious threat to the U.S. financial system.

As such, while it is impossible to quantify the degree to which insider trading helped to bring the U.S. financial system to its knees in 2008, there is no doubt that the practice has contributed to the contamination of the corporate and financial worlds' ethical cultures, setting criminal examples for others and providing grist for the psychological mill of rationalization that businesspeople in any sector of business could use to justify exploiting opportunities to profit by breaking the law.

And Then There Is AIG

Of all the corporate-level practitioners of deception during the period leading up to the financial crisis, AIG is arguably the trophy winner. It is also the most complex of the "players" in the meltdown story and it may be years before the tangled web of decisions, actions, rumors, accusations, and blatantly illegal business practices is sorted out to reveal the true story behind the company's 2008 implosion.

AIG was—and is—the subject of numerous legal actions alleging deceptive or unfair business practices, securities fraud, fraudulent financial reporting, and other serious violations. A few examples include:

- In 2003, AIG paid a $10 million civil penalty to settle fraud charges involving Plainfield, Indiana-based phone distributor Brightpoint Inc.
- In 2005, the company was sued by New York Attorney General Eliot Spitzer on charges of accounting fraud which, as discussed later in this chapter, led to the resignation of the firm's founder and former chairman, Maurice Greenberg.
- Greenberg and three other former AIG executives paid $115 million to settle a case brought by a Louisiana pension fund. The Teachers' Retirement System of Louisiana alleged that half of the $2.2 billion that AIG paid to C.V. Starr—a firm run by Greenberg that also underwrote some AIG business—from 2000 to 2005 was a sham, a way to artificially boost profits for AIG. They also questioned why some AIG executives were allowed to serve simultaneously as officers of Starr, while also profiting from business conducted between the two companies.

But the potentially costliest deception of all derived from the company's absurd "strategy" of writing billions of dollars worth of CDSs in the years prior to the meltdown, based on the flimsy assumption that home prices would continue to rise indefinitely.

The company's CDS activities were concentrated in its London-based affiliate, AIG Financial Products (AIG-FP) which between 2002 and 2007 was run by a man named Joseph Cassano. By the accounts of numerous published and unpublished sources, Cassano was an intense, control-driven, and at times abusive chief executive. According to several former AIG-FP employees, Cassano instilled fear in the organization through intimidation, outbursts of anger, and the liberal use of abusive language in lambasting employees.

Assuming such portrayals are accurate, it is likely that certain business decisions made in the London office were influenced by a Fuld/Mozilo-like personal ego-driven force on the part of Cassano. It is also likely that AIG-FP's business conduct crossed the line between legal and illegal, as evidenced by the fact that the UK Serious Fraud Office (SFO) opened a criminal investigation into the firm in early 2009. Details of the probe are sketchy; the SFO promptly adopted a closed mouth policy about the case. However it is known that the investigation, initiated in cooperation with the U.S. Department of Justice and the SEC, focused on what AIG itself told investors concerning "certain public disclosures, transactions, and practices of AIG and its subsidiaries" related to "AIG's valuation of and disclosures relating to the AIG-FP super senior credit default swap portfolio."[22]

Indeed it appears that one of the critical unanswered questions surrounding AIG's dramatic demise relates specifically to margin calls on these super senior credit defaults swaps (SSCDS) by counterparties such as Goldman Sachs and other large Wall Street firms. How AIG-FP responded to the margin calls in valuing the SSCDSs is the potential subject of fraud allegations. The reason appears to be, according to documents related to the matter, that Cassano may have attempted to misrepresent the true value of the contracts after the margin calls were received.

Evidence of this is contained in the response to a subpoena issued by the House Subcommittee on Oversight and Government Reform, to former AIG-FP's former Vice President of Accounting Policy, Joseph St. Denis. St. Denis stated that "I was concerned that the valuation model of at least one of AIG-FP SSCDS counterparties apparently indicated that AIG-FP was in a potentially material liability position."[23]

St. Denis went on to explain a distinctly irregular if not bizarre series of actions by Cassano that can be interpreted as an indirect reference to possibly fraudulent overstatement of the value of AIG-FP's SSCDS portfolio:

Despite my position ... I had no involvement with efforts to value AIG-FP's SSCDS portfolio. This was, in my understanding, due to the actions of Mr. Cassano to exclude me from the SSCDS valuation process. During the final week of September of 2007, the final week of my employment at AIG-FP, in a meeting with Mr. Cassano, the newly hired CFO of AIG-FP, and an AIG-FP quantitative risk expert, Mr. Cassano made the following statement to me: 'I have deliberately excluded you from the valuation of the Super Seniors because I was concerned that you would pollute the process.' My belief is that the 'pollution' Mr. Cassano was concerned about was the transparency I brought to AIG-FP's accounting policy process.

My understanding is that sometime during the late summer or early fall of 2007, AIG-FP executive and Credit Risk personnel began an effort to develop a so-called "Binomial Expansion Technique" (BET) model to provide valuations for the SSCDS portfolio that would reflect ongoing credit market developments. I had no involvement in this whatsoever other than attending a meeting held during the last week of September... during which the BET model was discussed. My knowledge of the process was gained solely from my attendance at this meeting. AIG's Controller, Director of Internal Audit, and Director of [the Office of Accounting Policy] attended this meeting held at AIG-FP's Wilton [Connecticut] office. During this meeting Mr. Cassano had one of the Risk Management people distribute a PowerPoint presentation that purported to show the application of the BET mode to AIG-FP's SSCDS portfolio and represented to the assembled group that the SSCDS portfolio continued to be in an aggregate unrealized gain position.[24]

St. Denis concludes his response with criticism of Cassano's allegedly misleading statement in December 2007 to AIG investors about the legitimacy of the margin calls on the SSCDS portfolio and on the actual value of that portfolio.

It is not easy to interpret the exact meaning of either St. Denis's or Cassano's various statements with regard to this specific matter. But it is reasonable to conclude that *something* of questionable legality or professional propriety was going on at AIG-FP during Cassano's reign. What the various investigative agencies ultimately conclude about this incident remains to be seen.

One party watching the development very closely is former New York Governor Eliot Spitzer. Spitzer was, during his tenure as State Attorney General, responsible for getting AIG founder and long-time CEO "Hank" Greenberg pushed out of the company by his own board in connection with the company's fraudulent financial reporting activities previously mentioned, involving the insurance company General Re.

Given the doggedness with which Spitzer pursued AIG on this and other instances of allegedly improper business conduct (including stock manipulation and tax evasion), it is not surprising that he would write in early 2009 that

Everybody is rushing to condemn AIG's bonuses [amounting to $165 million which was paid out of TARP money in late 2008], but this simple scandal is obscuring the real disgrace at the insurance giant: Why are AIG's [CDS] counterparties getting paid back in full, to the tune of tens of billions of taxpayer dollars? . . . The AIG bailout has been a way to hide an enormous second round of cash to the same group that had received TARP money already.

It all appears, once again, to be the same insiders protecting themselves against sharing the pain and risk of their own bad adventure. The payments to AIG's counterparties are justified with an appeal to the sanctity of contract. If AIG's contracts turned out to be shaky, the theory goes, then the whole edifice of the financial system would collapse.[25]

Spitzer's comments stop short of accusing AIG or its top executives of committing fraud in handling the CDS matter, but a class action lawsuit filed in Los Angeles does not. In that case, the plaintiffs charge AIG with, among other things, incurring huge losses as a result of its aggressive CDS portfolio growth which, according to the allegations, exceeded $350 billion in early 2008 and for which it was allegedly grossly undercapitalized in the event that the contracts triggered payment requirements by AIG, as they ultimately did in late 2008. The California case specifically alleges that "AIG's unlawful, fraudulent, and unfair business practices [with respect to its CDS activities] have reduced the capital, surplus, and reserves of [its] California insurance companies. AIG has used affiliated transactions and temporary paper transfers of funds to obscure the impact of the financial condition of the AIG California insurance companies."[26]

The bottom line is that the AIG fraud and ethics saga is lengthy and convoluted and is the subject of extensive legal and journalistic scrutiny. From the standpoint of unlawful conduct, though, the key issue is that the company has a rich history of deceptive, fraudulent, and unethical conduct. Its contribution to the 2007–2008 financial crisis is thus two-pronged: First, as an industry leader, AIG's long-term record of unsavory business conduct no doubt contributed to the degradation of American management ethics. Second, as a fanatical pursuer of outsized profits through blind excess (and potential fraud) in the CDS market, it played an instrumental role in bringing the entire financial system to the brink of collapse, ultimately saddling American taxpayers with a $185 billion bailout bill in the process.

How "Toxic" Securities Ended Up in So Many Investor Portfolios

If you refer to the discussion in Chapter 3 about how Bankers Trust essentially pulled the wool over the eyes of its trusting client, Gibson Greetings by concocting a bizarrely complex interest rate swap deal that ended up costing Gibson $1 million and earning BT $13 million, you'll realize that the practice of Wall Street firms of out-mathemetizing and sweet-talking clients into buying into deals they really don't understand is nothing new.

The same thing happened to Robert Citron in Orange County, California. That incident resulted in Merrill Lynch's payout of $400 million after being found by the courts to have outright scammed Orange County into purchasing securities it really didn't understand.

Similarly, in the period leading up to and during the crisis of 2007–2008, the problem of investor deception played no small role.

For example, in a 2008 crisis–related case, two securities brokers were convicted of charges in a case that the *New York Times* termed at the time of their indictment "a classic picture of greed and glory on Wall Street."[27] Eric Butler and Julian Tzolov, formerly of Credit Suisse, sold corporate clients securities backed by subprime mortgages, CDOs, and mobile home contracts. However, that is not what they told their clients who collectively bought about $820 million worth of these "securities." Instead, they told the clients that the securities were backed by student loans issued by an organization called Glacier Student Loan Authority and that these loans were "guaranteed by the U.S. Department of Education." What the brokers had *in fact* purchased and peddled to their unsuspecting clients were shares of "Glacier Funding CDO I Ltd," an entity that invested in risky securities, which in no way resembled secure government-guaranteed student loans. The deceptive sales were even more egregious because the clients of the two brokers had specifically instructed them to invest in safe government-guaranteed debt.

To cover up their crimes, committed between 2005 and 2007, Butler and Tzolov sent clients over 50 e-mails falsely describing the investments being sold to them as safe, government-backed, student loans.[28]

Butler was convicted and Tzolov pleaded guilty.

This and literally countless cases like it began clogging the court system in 2008. It will be years, according to the estimates of several experienced state and federal prosecutors, before these "meltdown-related" cases are finally resolved. The critical question for lawmakers, corporate executives, and investors is whether anything has been learned from these painful and costly misdeeds. This will be addressed in Chapter 8.

The Legalities of Deception

According to Bill Shepherd, founding partner of the Houston, Texas law firm of Shepherd, Smith, Edwards and Kantas, in making an investment recommendation to a client, a broker is required by law to make recommendations that are consistent with the customer's risk tolerance, needs, and investment objectives. Brokers have a duty to know their clients and to only recommend investments and trading strategies that are suitable for that client. It is this duty and the related legal standards, says Shepherd, that will form the grounds of many a plaintiff action against brokers and other marketers of high-risk derivative-based securities like Butler and Tzolov leading up to the meltdown.

For example, a particular investment may be unsuitable if a customer does not have the financial ability to incur the risk associated with that investment, if the investment was not in line with the investor's financial needs, *or if the customer did not know or understand risks associated with certain investments.*

A broker has a duty to gather essential information in order to understand the risk tolerance of an investor, the tax considerations for the client, the client's prior experiences and appetite for risk, and the level of return desired. It is the duty of a broker to make recommendations that are appropriate and suitable given his client's circumstances. If a broker breaches those duties and makes unsuitable recommendations for a client, the broker may be liable to that client.

The issue is not whether a broker picked the right stock, anyone can make a mistake, but whether the broker picked the right type of investment (for example, bonds and lower

(continued)

197

(*continued*)

risk stocks for a retirement account rather than high-risk stocks only).[29]

A broker must also have a "reasonable basis for the recommendation." The broker's basis for the recommendation can be the firm's research, in which case the firm must have a reasonable basis for its own recommendation.[30]

Rating Agency Deception Redux

As mentioned, according to several learned analysts, the lion's share of direct blame for the meltdown lies with the top executives of major banks, investment firms, and rating agencies. They charge the bank bosses with perpetuating a boom in reckless mortgage lending and the investment bankers by essentially tricking institutional investors into buying the exotic derivative securities backed by the millions and millions of "toxic" mortgages sold off by the mortgage lenders.

They were, according to these observers, aided and abetted by the rating agencies that lowered their rating standards on high-risk MBSs that should never have received investment-grade ratings, but did because the rating agencies receive their fees from the *issuers* of those bonds—that is, the investment banks. The agencies reportedly feared losing business if they gave poor ratings to the securities.

An apt summary of how the financial and government communities view the actions and attitudes of the three rating agencies in the years leading up to the subprime crisis can be found in a statement made during October 2008 hearings on the topic of rating agencies' role in the crisis by the House Committee on Oversight and Government Reform. During those hearings, the Committee cited a 2006 e-mail between agency analysts from a Standard & Poor's employee that contained such language as, "the rating agencies continue to create an even bigger monster, the CDO market. Let's hope we all are wealthy and retired by the time this house of cards falters."[31]

Committee member, Elijah Cummings summed up several hours of testimony by the three rating agency bosses by addressing the S&P employee's comment with this:

> *It seems to me that there was a climate [at the rating agencies] of mediocrity because when we go on, we realize that there were other people saying the same thing in your organization. Now although you may not think it reflected the culture, I think it reflected the culture, and my constituents think it reflected the culture, and to you Mr. [Raymond] McDaniel [Chairman of Moody's] you know this is your watch. You made a nice statement about your organization being around since 1909.*
>
> *But I wondered whether the folks who started your organization in 1909 would be happy with what they see today. Because there is, without a doubt, there has been a loss of trust. And somebody has to recover that. You have to get that trust back. We can never get these markets back, get them back right unless the investors feel comfortable about what is going on. And you're the gatekeepers. You're the guys. You're the ones that make all the money. You're there.*[32]

The thorny issue of conflict of interest with respect to the three major rating agencies and the derivative securities they were being paid to rate by the issuers themselves will not be easily resolved.

Most Wall Street observers familiar with the derivatives problem concur that the rating agencies were systemically conflicted and therefore had strong financial incentives to skew their ratings of CDO and other issuings higher than they should have been.

In one particularly outspoken assessment of the situation, author and former Wall Streeter John Talbott writes, "...in a move that makes no sense whatsoever, each of these rating agencies was paid by the issuer, not the investor, to double check the quality of the issuer's paper. And paid they were—sometimes as much as $50 million in fees for one issue of mortgage-backed securities." Talbott goes on to offer the analogy of a car dealer trying to sell a car to a customer who says he wants to independently check the condition of the vehicle and the salesman convinces the customer to save his money on hiring a mechanic and instead to just go to his brother-in-law who happens to be a mechanic.[33]

As one highly respected securities attorney with 40 years of experience representing maligned investors sums it up, "The rating agencies simply became whores in the early 2000s. There was too much money to be made by abandoning their independence and so that's exactly what they did."

There appears to be general consensus about this inherent conflict on the part of experts on the brokerage side of Wall Street. However, it is interesting to note that investment bankers who are far removed from the business of creating, marketing, and reaping massive commissions from the *trading* end of things have a much more positive opinion of the rating agencies. To them, it is incomprehensible that a rating agency would put its reputation on the line by fudging their ratings of securities issues. But then, investment bankers operate in a different world: Their job is to maintain strong relationships with corporate clients in order to get the underwriting business that these clients may generate. As such, the rating agencies have a more systematic and perhaps less corruption-prone role in rating the issuings of these entities.

Whether this caveat regarding the agencies is accurate or not is, however, academic with respect to their role in the derivatives rating business in the years leading up to the housing, securities, and credit market crashes of 2007–2008.

And So, The End Begins

In 2006 and 2007, three problems collided to bring down Lehman Brothers, Merrill Lynch, and AIG, three of the biggest "players" in the CDS market. First, the housing market went into free fall and homeowners started defaulting on their mortgages by the tens of thousands. That triggered demands by the buyers of CDSs to be paid on their contracts. Second, the mortgages which were going into default were almost impossible to identify because they had been carved up into pieces and mixed in with other parts of the mortgages as collateral for various forms of complicated securities. And third, the sellers of the CDSs—Merrill, Lehman, AIG, and others—had set aside no cash to make good on the contracts in the event that their bets went bad, as they did in mind-boggling proportions.

For several years leading up to the financial crisis, the unregulated markets for MBSs and CDSs appeared to run smoothly because none of the bets on which they were based went bad. That was principally because housing prices continued to rise and the risk of default on the underlying mortgages collateralizing the securities against which CDS contracts were written seemed increasingly remote.

But then the bubble burst and all those companies that had sold billions of dollars of CDS contracts were suddenly on the hook for these obligations which they had made no capital provision for. That is one of the prime reasons for the overnight collapse of Lehman Brothers, the near-collapse of Merrill Lynch (until it was scooped up at fire sale price by Bank of America), and AIG, which was able to hang on by a thread thanks to the magnanimity (or, political interests, according to many critics) of federal government decision makers ostensibly representing the U.S. taxpayer.

With the background of these emerging forces, as discussed in this and previous chapters, one would hope that the way in which they came together to bring the entire U.S. financial system to the brink of disaster would be relatively clear. However, details of the chain reaction that resulted in near-collapse in late 2007 are still being investigated. It may be years before the definitive story of the meltdown can be told.

Nonetheless, the role of fraud in all of this should now be starkly evident to readers. While not always directly related to the specific events of late 2007 and early 2008, fraud within U.S. corporations and government agencies and among banks, investment firms, and other financial institutions played a huge role, to say the least, in undermining the financial system and perhaps irreversibly compromising the country's business, political, and civic standards of ethics.

Notes

1. Frank Partnoy, *Infectious Greed: How Deceit and Risk Corrupted the Financial Markets* (New York: Henry Holt & Company, 2003), 374.
2. Charles R. Morris, *The Two Trillion Dollar Meltdown,* Charles R. Morris, Public Affairs (New York: Public Affairs, 2008), 74.
3. Ibid., 40.
4. Adam B. Ashcraft, "Measuring the Impact of Securitization on Imputed Bank Output," February 4, 2008. The details of the subprime securitization transaction cited by the authors are taken from the prospectus filed with the SEC and with monthly remittance reports filed with the Trustee. The former is available online using the Edgar database at www.sec.gov/edgar/searchedgar/companysearch.html with the company name GSAMP Trust 2006-NC2. The latter is available from www.absnet.net/.

5. Statement by New Jersey Attorney General Anne Milgram regarding the filing civil fraud suit against Richard Fuld, Lehman's Directors and its outside auditor, Ernst & Young, March 17, 2009, http://www.state.nj.us/governor/news/news/2009/approved/20090317b.html. Full complaint available at http://www.nj.gov/oag/newsreleases09/031709-nj-v-fuld.pdf.

6. Jessica Papini, "Lehman Doesn't See Large Write-Downs in Commercial Real Estate" *MarketWatch,* September 10, 2008, www.marketwatch.com.

7. Gillian Tett, *Fool's Gold* (New York: Free Press, 2009), 224.

8. William D. Cohan, *House of Cards* (New York: Doubleday, 2009), 247.

9. *United States v. Ralph Cioffi and Matthew Tannin,* U.S. District Court for the Eastern District of New York, June 18, 2008, Case # 1:08-cr-00415-FB.

10. Ibid.

11. Ibid.

12. Ibid.

13. William D. Cohan, "How the Scapegoats Escaped," *New York Times*, November 12, 2009, A35.

14. *In re: Washington Mutual, Inc.* Securities Litigation, No. 2:08-Md-1919 MJP, Lead Case No. C08-387 MJP, filed October 21, 2008, 343–344.

15. Paul Muolo and Mathew Padilla, *Chain of Blame: How Wall Street Caused the Mortgage and Credit Crisis* (Hoboken, NJ: John Wiley & Sons, 2008), 64–65.

16. Ibid., 87.

17. *Securities and Exchange Commission vs. Angelo Mozilo, David Sambol, and Eric Sieracki*, USDCCDC, cc09-09334.

18. Ibid.

19. Investopedia, www.investopedia.com/terms/s/shortswingprofit-rule.asp.

20. Thomas C. Newkirk, "Insider Trading: A U.S. Perspective," speech (Sept. 19, 1998), www.sec.gov/news/speech/speecharchive/1998/spch221.htm#FOOTNOTE_22.

21. Federal Defense Cases, www.federaldefensecases.com/treatise-article2.php.

22. Simon Bowers "Serious Fraud Office Investigates AIG," *Guardian*, February 12, 2009. www.guardian.co.uk/money/2009/feb/12/insurance-regulators.

23. Letter by Joseph St. Denis to House Subcommittee on Oversight and Government Reform, October 8, 2007.

24. Ibid.

25. Eliot Spitzer, "The Real AIG Scandal," *Slate*, March 17, 2009, www.slate.com/id/2213942/.

26. *Harris v. American International Group el al.*, Case #BC414205, Superior Court of California, Los Angeles.

27. Jenny Anderson, "Two Brokers Accused of Securities Fraud," *New York Times,* September 3, 2008.

28. *Securities and Exchange Commission v. Eric S. Butler and Julian T. Tzolov*, U.S.D.C. S.D.N.Y., Case #08-civ-7699, September 3, 2008.

29. Shepherd, Smith, Edwards & Kantas LLP, Houston, TX, www.stockbroker-fraud.com.

30. Shepherd, Smith, Edwards & Kantas LLP, Houston, TX, www.stockbroker-fraud.com/lawyer-attorney-1133449.html.

31. Securities and Exchange Commission, "Summary Report of Issues Identified in the Commission Staff's Examinations of Select Credit Rating Agencies," July, 2008, 12, http://www.sec.gov/news/studies/2008/craexamination070808.pdf.

32. Rep. Elijah Cummings, speaking at hearing, "Credit Rating Agencies and the Financial Crisis" Wednesday, October 22, 2008, House of Representatives, Committee on Oversight and Government Reform, Washington, D.C.

33. John T. Talbott, *Contagion* (Hoboken, NJ: John Wiley & Sons, 2009), 42.

CHAPTER 8

Can the Circle Be Broken?

A s should be abundantly evident from the foregoing chapter, it is impossible to identify a single overriding cause for the astounding permeation and brazenness of fraud and deception throughout the U.S. financial system in the years leading up to 2007. But it is equally clear that a woeful lack of government regulation of banking, insurance, and securities markets was high on the list of culprits.

Yet, in fairness to those whose jobs entail crafting laws and regulations aimed at safeguarding our financial institutions and the individuals and organizations they serve, it would have been difficult for even the sharpest of financial forecasters to predict that state and federal regulatory deficiencies would one day blow up in our faces in the form of a full-scale, indeed *global*, financial meltdown.

For that matter, is it reasonable to expect that our lawmakers and regulators should have seen the writing on the wall as the unalloyed greed and self-aggrandizement on the part of the Fulds, Mozilos, and others grew to unthinkable heights through the late 1990s and early 2000s, ultimately contributing mightily to the entire system's collapse?

What David Callahan, author of *The Cheating Culture* described as a new, cutthroat and ruthless financial culture beginning in the 1990s is the closest anyone came to forecasting the business community's moral and ethical decline that proved so poisonous to the financial markets in the early 2000s.

The FBI, however, deserves kudos for warning of the emerging epidemic of mortgage fraud back in 2004. Had regulators and responsible financial institution leaders heeded the Bureau's alarm, perhaps corrective measures would have been put in place to stave off the self-perpetuating marginalization of lending standards which caused the ill-fated subprime market to explode into the trillions of dollars within a few years.

But this is mere speculation, worthy only of providing ammunition for the multitudes of Monday morning quarterbacks who now profess to have the answer to the question of how we prevent a recurrence of the Great Crash of 2007–2008.

In fact there *is* no answer. There never can be one. History shows that the U.S. financial system is hard-wired for periodic crises and that regardless of how well-meaning and resolute the political leaders of the time, the best that can be hoped for is a post-trauma flurry of legal and regulatory reform that at best temporarily mitigates, but can never eliminate the risk of a future disaster.

Without a doubt, the most realistic and effective set of such remedial laws and regulations on record emerged from the Depression of the 1930s. As discussed, Glass-Steagall in particular ensured that banking, insurance, and investment banking firms remained separate and apart from each other and thus unable to accumulate so much financial might that they would become essentially impossible to regulate and, in contemporary parlance, too big to fail.

With the benefit of hindsight it is now obvious that since 1999 the financial services industry took full advantage of its newfound freedom. Indeed, in the course of doing so, Wall Street initiated a *tsunami* of progressively more complex derivative products that flourished below the regulatory radar. It was only a matter of time before financial institutions souped up their money machinery to securitize anything they could create a market for regardless of the risk levels and, it should be added, with less and less transparency. Yet customers were being pushed increasingly hard to buy these "attractive" and purportedly safe investments. Whether the buyers knew it or not (and too often they did not), the more of these "securities" they bought, the greater the risk they were exposing their portfolios to.

Similarly, the 1933 empowerment of the Securities and Exchange Commission (SEC) to police the securities markets proved for many decades to be a better-than-nothing stopgap against unbridled fraud, abuse, and deception on the part of investment industry players. The embarrassing failure to catch the history-making Bernard Madoff scam notwithstanding, the SEC's general record of catching securities fraudsters has not been all that terrible.

Thus, with the 1995 enactment of the Private Securities Litigation Reform Act, which effectively hog-tied many prospective investor-litigants from pursuing justice in cases of major investment rip-offs, and the 1999 repeal of Glass-Steagall which opened the floodgates of mega-banking, the legal and regulatory stage was set for an inevitable financial crisis of unprecedented proportion.

So What Now?

As the powerful chairman of the House Committee on Financial Services, Barney Frank of Massachusetts told National Public Radio in August 2009, getting a consensus on a meaningful financial services regulatory reform bill *must* happen within a matter of months—not years. Importantly, however, in the same interview, he was unable to predict how or what kind of consensus would ultimately emerge.

This tells us that the debate over how to reshape the stupendously defective regulatory system now in place will drag on indefinitely. It may be that the best that can be hoped for is a series of "mini" reforms spanning the course of several years. Either way, there certainly is no shortage of ideas and proposals for reform, some more likely than others to secure the political support needed to make it through the legislative minefield in Washington.

Thus, without attempting to predict the unpredictable, it is hoped that the reader will be best served at this point by a list of the major issues requiring reform, along with synopses of the more realistic and potentially most promising proposals put forward thus far for restoring financial stability and preventing fraud.

Critical Reform Issues

Regardless of the political climate in Washington, the most pressing need for reform exists in the following areas:

Asset Securitization and Derivatives Trading

The widely-lauded "innovativeness" of Wall Street which is equated with the natural source of efficiency and adaptiveness of the U.S. financial system is clearly a treasured benefit that no politician would dare tinker with. The problem is that in too many instances during the 1990s and early 2000s, innovativeness became synonymous with complexity and excessive risk. The unregulated introduction of complicated mortgage and other asset-backed securities such as collateralized debt obligations (CDOs), collateralized mortgage obligations (CMOs), mortgage-backed securities (MBSs), and the like had great value in terms of adding liquidity to the credit markets. But left as they were to their own devices, the deal makers and marketers of these securities sucked in unwitting institutional and individual investors who were led to believe—often through blatantly fraudulent sales tactics—that they were buying into high-yield instruments that were safer than they actually were, thus adding fuel to the real estate bubble that so violently burst. Some of the more sober reform proposals on the table are summarized as follows:

Former Federal Reserve (Fed) Board Co-Chair Alice Rivlin, now at the Brookings Institution, proposed formation of what she terms a "Macro System Stabilizer" (MSS). This entity would have what Rivlin terms "broad responsibility for the entire financial system charged with spotting perverse incentives, regulatory gaps, and market pressures that might destabilize the system and taking steps to fix them."[1]

Rivlin makes a convincing case for such an entity by pointing out that lax lending standards resulted in huge volumes of "bad mortgages" being approved and then securitized into the toxic assets that essentially put the balance sheets of major financial institutions on life support.

According to Rivlin, "lax lending standards by mortgage originators should have been spotted as a threat to stability by a Macro System Stabilizer—the Fed should have played this role and failed to do so—and corrected by tightening the rules (minimum down payments, documentation, proof that the borrow understands the terms of the loan and other no-brainers)."[2]

Presumably, a Macro System Stabilizer such as this could have identified the incentives on the part of mortgage brokers and lenders to defraud unqualified borrowers by pushing them into loans they were incapable of repaying. In other words, a Rivlin-like stabilizing entity could moderate lender and broker greed by establishing laws and regulations that prohibit irresponsible (and/or predatory) lending.

As for the securitization part of the equation, Rivlin proposes that loan originators be required to maintain a certain (unspecified) percentage of all the mortgages they write. She suggests that the Obama Administration's proposal that this figure be set at 5 percent is too low, but she does support the concept, as it would in theory reduce the incentive for securitizing institutions to bundle "junk" loans into securities that could later backfire on them.

This and other bank-related regulatory reform will no doubt be strenuously resisted by the powerful banking lobby. The American Bankers Association (ABA) for instance vociferously opposes any major new regulation. It specifically aims its formidable political arsenal at the Obama Administration's proposed Consumer Financial Products Agency (CFPA), arguing that there are already numerous laws and regulations protecting consumers from unscrupulous or unfair banking practices. ABA President and CEO Edward Yingling testified at a Congressional hearing that "It is simply unfair to inflict another burden on these banks that had nothing to do with the problems that were created. The separate consumer regulator will only add costs to these banks—which already suffer under the enormous regulatory burden placed on them."[3]

Reading between the lines, it is clear that Yingling blames the Countrywides and other nondepository lenders for all of the country's financial woes. Whether that is a reasonable assessment is a matter of opinion.

However, it is interesting that in the same session, Yingling told the legislators that "Traditional FDIC-insured banks—more than any other financial institution class—are dedicated to delivering consumer financial services right the first time and have the compliance programs and top-down culture to prove it."[4]

This begs the question of why the FDIC was forced to seize over 80 failed banks in the first nine months of 2009, compared with only 25 for all of 2008, 3 in 2007, and *none* in 2006.

The bottom line is that the Obama Administration has a tough row to hoe in its efforts to accomplish meaningful banking reform that truly stabilizes the industry for the long term.

Mortgage Broker and Appraiser Regulation

One of the chief deterrents for independent mortgage brokers and appraisers to falsify mortgage application information is the prospect of criminal prosecution. As former U.S. Associate Deputy Attorney General Kevin O'Connor predicts, many of the unscrupulous brokers and appraisers who operated without impunity through most of the 2000s should, and probably will be charged with violating state consumer protection and/or state bank-fraud laws.

A much needed long-term solution to the crooked broker problem will require implementation of a regulatory regime for this industry. Hopefully preceding chapters have demonstrated that the absence of such rules is now widely blamed for the widespread greed-driven frauds committed by so many of these independent businesspeople in the years leading up to the fateful days and weeks of late 2007.

Former mortgage lender Richard Bitner points out the need for a law requiring brokers to fully disclose all fees applicable to loans being offered to borrowers as well as a requirement that brokers disclose to borrowers how much money they will make on a proposed loan. This, suggests Bitner, would result in brokers being required to educate borrowers about the specific roles and compensation of brokers and lenders.[5]

Bitner, along with other promoters of reform, also strongly urges Congress to implement a requirement for brokers and appraisers to be licensed and accredited. Ideally, this rule would be similar to those applicable to certified public accountants and licensed financial advisors. These professionals are required to pass rigorous tests that measure their familiarity with their fiduciary obligations and the ethical standards that must be adhered to in order to maintain accreditation. Mandatory continuing education, like that required of CPAs and attorneys wouldn't be a bad idea for mortgage brokers and appraisers as well.

Bank Lending Standards and Capital Requirements

Virtually no one outside of the Obama Administration agrees that there should be a "too-big-to-fail" safety net in the form of federal bailout. There are plenty of reasons to oppose this, perhaps most compelling, the argument that doing so would establish a damaging moral hazard in bailing out firms that have reached the brink by making irresponsible lending and investing decisions. Doing so would implicitly reduce the incentive for other large institutions to conduct their affairs in financially prudent ways, knowing that the safety net awaits if they stray.

Among the most simple and straightforward proposals for finally ending the unwinnable argument over the "too-big-to-fail" concept as it applies to such unmanageable behemoths as JP Morgan, AIG, Bank of America, Wells Fargo, and Citigroup comes in the form of a question from former Goldman Sachs Managing Director, Nomi Prins: ". . . why not bust up AIG into an insurance component and a trading component, pull a Glass-Steagall on this insurance company cloaked in a savings and loan wrap, and then after that's done, why not do the same thing to every other mega-bank to create a more manageable financial system for the sake of our collective future economic stability?"[6]

As this book goes to press, the proposals for stabilizing large lending institutions are numerous and varied. Almost certainly, a complete repeal of Glass-Steagall is a political nonstarter. It is more realistic to expect a "surgical" revision of the Act, possibly reverting to a degree of functional segregation between commercial banking, investment banking, and insurance that would at least limit the opportunity for financial institutions to drive themselves to the point of no return, with only the federal government capable of forestalling collapse.

No doubt some form of a watered-down rule requiring higher minimum capital reserves and other stopgap measures for banks will emerge from Washington. It remains to be seen, however, whether additional *meaningful* legal and regulatory safeguards against reckless and destructive lending practices will—or even can—be promulgated.

Rating Agency Reform

As discussed in Chapter 7, there is widespread consensus that the three main rating agencies, S&P, Moody's, and Fitch were less than objective in setting ratings for many MBSs, including subprime-backed issuings.

There is as yet little statistical support for the argument that because the issuers are compensated for their services by the financial institutions whose securities they are rating, they cannot therefore be objective. But there is equally little dispute of the argument, except of course from the rating agencies themselves.

Importantly though, even the Fed, in a meticulously researched and highly technical study entitled "Understanding the Securitization of Subprime Mortgage Credit," concluded that:

> *The rating agencies are paid by the arranger and not investors for their opinion, which creates a potential conflict of interest. The opinion is arrived at in part through the use of models (about which the rating agency naturally knows more than the investor), which are susceptible to both honest and dishonest errors.*[7]
>
> *Our view is that the rating of securities, secured by subprime mortgage loans, by credit rating agencies has been flawed. There is no question that there will be some painful consequences.*[8]

The authors, however, propose no further regulation of the credit agencies, suggesting that they are taking "remedial steps in the right direction."

Whether this proves accurate remains to be seen.

Risk Management

The Obama Administration's proposal for preventing another situation in which financial institutions over-leverage themselves with unregulated derivatives boils down to this:

> *We propose to bring the markets for all OTC derivatives and asset-backed securities into a coherent and coordinated regulatory framework that requires transparency and improves market discipline. Our proposal would impose record keeping and reporting requirements on all OTC derivatives. We also propose to strengthen the prudential regulation of all dealers in the OTC derivative markets and to reduce systemic risk in these markets by requiring all standardized OTC derivative transactions to be executed in regulated and transparent venues and cleared through regulated central counterparties.*[9]

Unfortunately, the Obama proposal offers little detail on how this rather attractive-sounding regulatory framework would be achieved other than to suggest that gaps in regulation of these instruments that currently exist between the SEC and the Commodity Futures Trading Commission (CFTC) should be eliminated.

There is broad consensus on the desirability of greater transparency and tighter regulation of the derivatives products that played such a devastating role in bringing down the financial system in 2007–2008. Whether a politically acceptable plan for doing so can be devised remains to be seen.

Among the more thoughtful proposals for achieving realistic and effective derivatives regulation is the one offered by John Coffee, PhD, and Hillary Sale, PhD, distinguished law professors at Columbia University. Coffee and Sale base their reform proposal on a succinct and instructive summarization of the genesis of the financial crisis:

> *In retrospect, irresponsible lending in the mortgage market appears to have been a direct response to the capital markets' increasingly insatiable demand for financial assets to securitize. If underwriters were willing to rush deeply flawed asset-backed securitizations to the market, mortgage loan originators had no rational reason to resist them.*
>
> *Thus, the real mystery is not why loan originators made unsound loans, but why underwriters bought them.*[10]

Coffee and Sale conclude that the main reason for the "mystery" is a severe breakdown in regulation. In fact they state that "failures in regulatory oversight...may have played a greater causal role in the debacle than has been generally emphasized."[11]

The suggestion offered by Coffee and Sale to remedy the problem of regulatory failure in the area of bank risk-taking includes giving broad authority to a new consolidated federal agency, presumably a somewhat reconstituted Fed. Specifically, they suggest that "For the future, it seems obvious that financial regulators will need to restrict leverage and risky trading practices, both at investment banks and other financial institutions ...The best [entities to accomplish this are] banking regulators [who] have better skilled personnel (and more of them), better information (acquired from their regulatory oversight of commercial banks and other financial institutions), and greater power over their regulated institutions."[12]

More to the point of this book—preventing fraud from destabilizing the financial system—it has been proposed by many observers that the federal securities laws that currently govern stocks be extended to apply to derivatives, especially CDOs.

As Richard Mendales, J.D., a visiting professor at Penn State University School of Law convincingly points out, "fraud in connection with the sale of mortgages or other non-securitized debt obligations is subject primarily to state law. Since this sale is now largely made for the purpose of securitization, it makes sense to subject fraud in such transactions to uniform federal regulation, as it did to federalize the law of fraud in connection with the sale of securities. Ginnie Mae already protects its guaranties by requiring each issuer whose securities it guaranties to post a fidelity bond, to protect against losses caused by 'dishonest, fraudulent, or negligent acts' by officers, employees, or other agents of the issuer, and insurance against errors and omissions by the issuer's officers, employees, and agents. For private label issuers, the antifraud and due diligence requirements of the securities laws would substitute for these bonds."[13]

Mendales hits the proverbial nail on the head by proposing that civil or criminal action be initiated against any institution that actively deceives the investing public in its CDO dealings. He suggests that the SEC's enforcement division take the lead in civil cases, as it already does with more conventional securities, but that criminal action be pursued in instances where prosecution is warranted. While perhaps not a silver bullet, this regulatory change would eliminate the earlier-referenced "free-for-all" that investment firms enjoyed in pushing the CDO market to the point of ubiquitous and outright deception of prospective investors.

To reinforce this anti-fraud measure, Mendales also proposes that:

> . . . *the sale of a debt instrument with knowledge that it would be securitized, accompanied by a material misrepresentation concerning the instrument sold, should be made a violation of the antifraud provisions of the federal securities laws. The SEC's Enforcement Division is better organized to enforce*

such provisions than most states or the scattered U.S. Attorney's offices across the country. Its experience ranges from administrative actions to litigation, and extends to international transactions, which are outside the scope of state agencies or U.S. Attorney's offices.[14]

Mendales has equally harsh solutions to the credit default swap (CDS) and rating agency problems. For example, he proposes that current legal restrictions on the SEC over regulation of the CDS market be repealed and that the SEC also be given substantive legal powers to enforce what the Securities Act of 1933 already calls for: requiring the rating agencies to meet "an appropriate due diligence standard, at least with regard to ratings that issuers pay them to provide as part of the initial issuance of structured finance securities."[15]

Mendales offers a further series of specific due diligence standards and procedures for eliminating the problem of inadequate if not decidedly poor rating agency due diligence regarding the quality of mortgages and other securities being used to create derivative instruments.

Borrower Fraud ("Liar Loan" Deterrence and Punishment)

As could have been expected, the widespread problem of no-documentation, or "liar's loans," has at least temporarily self-corrected as lenders have, through the forces of self-preservation, stopped approving loan applications without income/employment verification.

However, the question remains of how to prevent these fraudulent loans from reappearing once memories of the meltdown have faded. The obvious answer is to toughen criminal penalties for lying on a mortgage application and, most importantly, to *enforce* the law. In addition, any bank that knowingly approves a loan containing false information should be fined.

Some observers have gone so far as to propose that the government offer bounties to whistle-blowers who report illegal conduct by brokers or borrowers. The concept is highly controversial. On the other hand, the federal government pays handsomely for information provided to it about waste and abuse by federal contractors. So perhaps paying for information about incidents of mortgage fraud would act as a deterrent to folks who might otherwise think nothing of submitting a grossly fictitious loan application to a broker or lender.

Financial Industry Cultural Reform

Of all the proposed legal, regulatory, and industry standards swirling around the halls of legislative houses at all levels of government, none address the one weakness in our business and financial systems which contributed most profoundly to the crisis of 2007–2008: The inexorable fraying of the formidable ethical fabric and unwritten rules of integrity upon which all of the country's business, social, and civic institutions were built.

Once unbridled greed and self-interest became the guiding drivers of business conduct in the financial markets, there was no longer any hope that a calamity of the kind experienced in 2007–2008 could possibly have been averted.

Closely connected to the greed factor of course were the obsessive and bloated egos of Wall Street bosses which set an example for the infectious mindset of "anything goes" among securities traders, managers, and sales representatives. Mortgage brokers, lenders, and other "support" players quickly got swept along by the irreversible undertow of corruption.

Whatever dignity and decorum that Wall Street possessed prior to the 1990s was slowly but steadily dismantled as the drive for instant riches consumed the financial markets, bringing them closer to disaster with every passing year.

As Patricia Harned, PhD, President of the respected Ethics Resource Center wrote:

> *History tells us the entire thrust of the federal government's approach [to the financial crisis] will be compliance-based. It's what lawmakers and regulators do. Part of the ritual is to write new rules that this time will* really *stick it to the bad actors. . . . The House and Senate will . . . work on major re-writes of the entire financial regulatory corpus ("re-reg" is the term of art). . . . Executive branch agencies, meanwhile, have been in high enforcement mode for months.*
>
> *The catch is that strict reporting of financial data tells only part of the story. And it follows that a lot of heat and light in making the rules more expansive and enforcement ever-tighter does not take us to the heart of the problem. Of course, there is no foolproof system, humans being human. But there is a better way than relying entirely on objective reporting of financial details.*
>
> *[Ethics Resource Center] research shows that a rules-based ethics program is essential in an organization. A principles-based* ethical culture *also demonstrably reduces misconduct. When a company or agency combines the two, they do themselves a big favor . . . The lack of focus on measurable ethical culture activities is a chronic blind spot in the government's perspective.*
>
> *In ERC's experience, an ethical culture is one in which the directors and top management take ethics seriously and work to embed ethical values in the organization; middle management supervisors reinforce and respect the values, and peers on the factory floor get the message that "that's how it's done around here."*
>
> *Ethical culture metrics, then, should track the danger of conflicts of interest at the board and senior management*

*levels—especially now that taxpayer dollars are flowing in the
veins of many a bank, auto maker, mortgage company, and
stimulus recipient. Metrics should help uncover corporate systems that encourage excessive risk-taking by CEOs and other
top executives, rewarding short-term gains and a boost in the
stock price at the expense of long-term stability and growth.
Measures should be taken of whether the culture encour-
ages whistle-blowing or permits retaliation against those who
report wrongdoing.*

*Collecting and analyzing survey data on ethical culture,
as well as traditional auditing and accounting safeguards,
is an idea whose time needs to be coming soon. If it does, it
may help tamp down the fire next time.*[16]

Policing, Policy, and Propriety

History shows that financial scoundrels will always get away
with as much as the absence of preventive or punitive policies, laws, and regulations allows. But the epidemic of legal
corner-cutting that spread throughout virtually every corner of
financial, corporate, civic, governmental, and community institutions in the years leading up to the disastrous months between
September 2007 and late 2008 amply demonstrates that America's fraud problem is far more complex and profound than the
mere mechanics of unlawful financial activity on Wall Street and
Main Street in that period.

Rather, as discussed in Chapter 2, and reiterated previously
by Dr. Harned, the fraud *culture* that has come to define American life must be confronted, dismantled, and replaced with a
modern version of the ethical and moral pillars upon which
American greatness was built. Without that, the ethical and moral
underpinnings of our business institutions will remain cracked
and crippled, giving financial criminals continued run of the
house.

America has long been a cultural paradox encompassing good, bad, and in between, with good for the most part dictating the important choices made by its citizenry, its political leadership, and its cultural leaders.

But the paradox has shifted. The bad and the in-between have gained ground in recent years and that is why the statistics show dramatic increases in fraud of *all* kinds.

Against that backdrop, it becomes clear that the remedy for America's ethical malady must be one of multiple approaches on multiple levels.

Notes

1. Testimony of Alice M. Rivlin, "Establishing a Framework for Systemic Risk Regulation," U.S. Senate Committee on Banking, Housing and Urban Affairs, July 23, 2009.
2. Ibid.
3. Testimony of Edward L. Yingling on behalf of the American Bankers Association before the Committee on Financial Services, United States House of Representatives, June 24, 2009.
4. Ibid.
5. Richard Bitner, *Confessions of a Subprime Mortgage Lender: An Insider's Tale of Greed, Fraud, and Ignorance* (Hoboken, NJ: John Wiley & Sons, 2008), 162.
6. Nomi Prins, *It Takes a Pillage* (Hoboken, NJ: John Wiley & Sons, 2009), 191.
7. Adam B. Ashcraft and Til Schuermann, "Understanding the Securitization of Subprime Mortgage Credit," Federal Reserve Bank of New York (Staff Report no.318 March, 2008), ii, www.newyorkfed.org/research/staff_reports/sr318.pdf.
8. Ibid, p. 66.
9. Department of the Treasury, "Financial Regulatory Reform, a New Foundation Rebuilding Financial Supervision and Regulation," June 17, 2009, 6.

10. John C. Coffee, Jr., Adolf A. Berle, and Hillary A. Sale, "Redesigning the SEC: Does the Treasury Have a Better Idea?" *Virginia Law Review* 95 (June 2009): 734.
11. Ibid.
12. Ibid., 778.
13. Richard E. Mendales, J.D., "Collateralized Explosive Devices: Why Securities Regulation Failed to Prevent the CDO Meltdown, and How to Fix It," Research Paper No. 09-2009, 71–72.
14. Ibid.
15. Ibid., 75.
16. Patricia Harned, "Financial Crisis: Living With the Legacy," September 2, 2009, www.ethics.org/ethics-today/0909/pat-column.html.

About the Author

Peter Goldmann is the president of White-Collar Crime 101 LLC, the publisher of *White-Collar Crime Fighter,* a monthly newsletter for internal auditors, controllers, corporate counsel, financial operations managers, and fraud investigators.

Peter has published *White-Collar Crime Fighter* since 1998 and has interviewed hundreds of fraud investigators, forensic accountants, white-collar crime attorneys, ex-convicts, and auditors.

In addition, White-Collar Crime 101 has developed the leading employee fraud awareness training program, *FraudAware.* This is a user-friendly workshop, Webinar, and E-learning training tool designed to educate employees at all levels in how to detect, prevent, and report incidents of fraud or suspicious conduct.

The course, which is customized for individual corporate, non-profit, and government agency clients, reinforces companies' whistleblowing programs, by enabling employees to detect fraudulent activity that can then be reported to supervisors or managers or by using the organization's confidential hotline.

Peter has 25 years of experience as a business journalist and trainer, having launched, edited, and published numerous business trade periodicals covering small business, international trade, management strategy, banking, and personal finance. He is a member of the Editorial Advisory Committee of the

Association of Certified Fraud Examiners (ACFE) as well as an active member of the Institute of Internal Auditors, the High-Tech Crime Investigation Association, and InfraGard.

He is a regular columnist for the ACFE's newsletter, *The Fraud Examiner*, and is a frequent contributor to other leading industry publications on anti-fraud topics. He has appeared on *The Wall Street Journal This Morning*, Fox Business News, *The New York Times*, and *Internal Auditor* magazine.

He can be reached at pgoldmann@wccfighter.com.

Index